The Ultimate Legacy

Published with the
Sponsorship and Support of

Family Enterprise Institute™

The Ultimate Legacy

How Owners
of Family and Closely Held Businesses
Can Achieve Their Real Purpose

Donald J. Jonovic, Ph.D.

Jamieson Press
Cleveland

Published by JAMIESON PRESS

Post Office Box 909, Cleveland, Ohio 44120

Library of Congress Cataloging in Publication Data

Jonovic, Donald J. 1943-

The ultimate legacy : how owners of family and closely held businesses can achieve their real purpose / Donald J. Jonovic. — 1st ed.

p. cm.

Includes index.

ISBN 0-915607-13-1

1. Family-owned business enterprises—United States—Management.
2. Close Corporations—United States—Management.
I. Title.

HD62.25.J664 1997 658'.045—dc21 96-37761 CIP

First Edition: January 1997

This book is dedicated to Sally Thérèse Gerster, my grandniece, and new hope for a new century; Dr. James J. Ackmann, a lifelong friend and current inspiration; and Joseph and Ann Jonovic, my parents, whose legacy is still unfolding.

Contents

TODAY

APPENDICES

Acknowledgements

This book has been in the "formative" stages for more than ten years. Since writing *Someday It'll All Be Yours...Or Will It?* in 1982, I've been fortunate in developing satisfying and productive long-term working relationships with a number of client companies. Together we have built successful techniques and approaches and collected an expanding body of experience and information, which I have long hoped to bring to a wider audience.

Desire and accomplishment, as most business owners know, are two different things, however. It took a series of meetings with executives at the Family Enterprise Institute™, particularly Charles W. Grover and Roger J. Warrum, to give me both the impetus and the support needed to dedicate the time necessary to write this book.

Few, if any, useful ideas spring solely from one individual. Credit for whatever practicality and effectiveness is found on these pages must be shared with my clients, many of whom have become respected friends over the years, and, with whom, most of these ideas were developed and "field tested."

Among them (and it is impossible to recognize everyone) are William H. Darr of American Dehydrated Foods, Springfield, Missouri; Ernest D. Key, Jnr., of the Atlanta Belting Co., Atlanta, Georgia; Webb and Scott Cooper and Joseph Abramczyk of Belting Industries, Kenilworth, New Jersey; Clyde and Paul Snodgrass, of

Clark-Snodgrass Co., Toledo, Ohio; Jack Day of Graphic World Printing Co., Cleveland, Ohio; James D. Olson, Brownlee Cote and all the members of the extended Cote family of Etoc Corp., Minneapolis, Minnesota; Ray Zukowski, Michele Canty, Ken Wakeen, and Robert Garon of Euclid Industries, Cleveland, Ohio; Jack Shaffer, John Gill and Rita Williams of Gill Industries, Grand Rapids, Michigan; Joel Marx and John Geller of Medical Services Co., Cleveland, Ohio; Carolyn Martin, Jan Sidley, Robert Sidley, and John Monroe of R.W. Sidley Inc., Painesville, Ohio; and William E. Spengler, Sr., of Tolco Corp., Toledo, Ohio.

Ideas are often intellectual "partnerships." Many colleagues added greatly to my understanding of these issues, particularly Malvin E. Bank, James E. Barrett, Theodore H. Cohn, Léon A. Danco, and Ernesto J. Poza.

In boardrooms, where the bullets fly and theory becomes practice having real effects on real lives, I have benefited from the experience and wisdom of fellow directors, particularly Frank S. Doyle, Jeff Grover, James Hooker, Walter W. Faster, Kenneth Kensington, Dale Lytkowski, John Warfel, Ed Waters, and James Weaver.

Special thanks are owed to George Santa, Donald Santa, Norman Santa, and John Santa, to Ronald Case Sharp, and my fellow directors on the Santa Holding Co. Board, Paul R. Ruby and Dean M. Hottle, II, for their contribution to developing the concepts behind the retirement planning model in *Appendix A-11*. Also, particular credit is owed to Bob Purcell, Nick Schomaker, D.J. McVicar, and Randy Green of Atlanta Belting Co. for helping to develop the profit-based incentive compensation system summarized in *Appendix A-3*.

Most central and fundamental of all has been the unwavering support, insightful advice, penetrating critique and persistent focus on quality I've enjoyed from my business partner, best friend, and spouse, Pamela McNeil Jonovic.

Foreword

Why, with all the frustrations, stresses, demands, and risks involved, do we choose to continue owning and running a business?

- Because it's a source of ever-increasing cash flow?

- Because it provides dividends and distributions?

- Because we — and our heirs and descendants — can operate and manage it?

- Because it gives us influence and power in our community?

- Because it's a launching platform for growth and acquisition?

- Because we can eventually sell it or go public?

- Because...?

We each can fill in our own blanks. The conceivable reasons for staying committed to a specific business are, in fact, as varied as the population of business owners. Further, the more owners there are *within* a given business, the more objectives and needs that business must fill. Consequently, with business success and the passage of time, the potential for complexity and confusion within a closely held business increases dramatically, particularly with respect to business purpose.

A lot of time, energy, and emotion is expended by owners, directors, managers, and advisors as they attempt to sort out this confusion and reduce the conflict it feeds, all too often with little success. I know, because I've fought those battles, in my own business and alongside the clients I serve. It took a while to realize why we weren't always as effective as we wanted to be.

What these struggles and resulting scars teach us is the critical need to cut beneath the complexities of current business challenges and varied personal goals to a more important objective: defining a commonly shared central *purpose* and then managing our business to achieve that purpose. This agreement is what will enable us, as owners, to maintain joint commitment to our businesses despite the stress, frustration, and risk we face every day.

While the nature of this real purpose is not difficult to understand, it is hard to agree on its specific definition, and almost impossible to keep in focus while we're dancing around bullets in the heat of battle. Nevertheless, this is precisely what we must do. Because beneath all the logos, product lines, price lists, and organization charts, beyond all the daily challenges from personnel issues to government regulations, *a business is an investment of precious capital* (not only money, but also valuable time, energy, ideas, concern, and commitment), *for the purpose of achieving an acceptable return on that investment.*

Obvious? Perhaps. But obvious or not, the reality is that too many of us aren't guided by this fundamental direction on our business compass. And it's precisely our failure to achieve agreement on this underlying purpose that is the central cause of conflict among owners of closely held businesses. It has, in fact, destroyed more businesses than all the external market challenges combined.

There's an old saw in agriculture about the farmer who won $3 million in the state lottery. When asked by a reporter what he planned to do with the money, he replied: "That's easy. I'm going to use it to farm, and I'll keep farming 'til it's gone."

Rings a bell, doesn't it? His reasons for farming—the independent life style, the love of the land, etc.—were so powerful that he put his love of the business ahead of the need for profitability.

Well, who's to say a business can't be used as a self-supporting hobby or terminal cash cow? Those are, after all, forms of return on investment. The particular definition isn't as important as the need for the owner or owners to know what they're doing, and agree on it.

Where business owners run into serious trouble is in situations where there are conflicting definitions of "returns" either vying for attention in the mind of a sole owner or causing disagreements among multiple owners who have greatly differing definitions of "acceptable return" and/or "investment." The existence of these conflicts, whether for a sole owner struggling in his own confusion or among multiple owners who fail to agree, is what so often leads to failure, ultimately, to achieve any reasonable return at all.

The bad news is that defining and agreeing on "investment" and "acceptable return" (which, together, I refer to in this book as "owner value") is not that simple. Still, the good news is that, when defined carefully and managed well, the owner value of a closely held business can significantly exceed financial value alone.

Owner value can be *defined* many ways by business owners, but in order to be preserved, it must, in fact, *be* defined. Owner value may be defined as ever-increasing cash flow. It can be large distributions. It can be owner-management. It can be economic and social influence. It can be acquisition and growth. It can even be sale of the business and investment in tax-free municipals. Actually, owner value in most private businesses is financial return *plus* a spectrum of other value components upon which owners usually fail to agree.

This failure to agree upon, and manage, the real purpose of business ownership is the fundamental cause of failure in family and closely held businesses.

Without this agreement about owner value — ultimately, an

agreement about purpose — owners will almost inevitably disagree on results and direction, boards will remain fictional or paralyzed, managers will drift and dissipate essential energies, and the business will fail to respond to challenges in the business environment.

This book focuses on achieving this definition. It looks at the sources of difference among owners, at ways of getting the right help to resolve those differences, and ways to manage the process of achieving and maintaining agreement.

It is the preservation of this jointly accepted owner value, not just successful management and transition of a business, that will become the ultimate legacy of the business owner.

Introduction: The Keys to Managing Owner Value

Mike Jensen looked up at the frayed Christmas banner above the door to his office. An edge curled where the tape had lost its hold, dried out from the old building's hyper-heated air.

The headache still sat on his shoulder, probing his knotted muscles.

Thirty years of work. For this...

His son, Jenks, had just stormed out, ranting at Mike's insensitivity to his righteous complaint, whatever it was. Mike couldn't remember, really. There were so many.

The real issue this night, the source of the headache, was a major customer, ABL Industries, who accounted for 20% of Mike's sales volume.

"We got a quote from one of your competitors," ABL's purchasing guy had called that morning to tell him. He was sincere. Even regretful (*right!*). "You guys were Supplier of the Year, excellent quality, good service. We've had a great relationship. Goes back 20 years.

"But," he added, "they've offered a 15% lower price, Mike."

Mike knew he'd keep the business. No question of that. But now the groveling began. Service. Quality. JIT. All those great fantasies airbrushed in *Fortune* management fold-outs usually boiled down to margin shavings on the controller's floor.

Mike looked around his office. The picture of him with Reagan — maybe the guy *was* a little vague, but Mike could never avoid smiling in his presence. Next to Reagan, the family pictures. The grandkids, all eight of them. He couldn't stop *that* smile, either.

He looked at the old, framed certificates, AMA "Strategic Management," that sort of thing, and an empty sense of loss washed over him. Only yesterday, the colors were sharp and fresh. He and his two brothers had left the GM plant full of enthusiasm, naiveté, guts and a touch of stupidity, certain beyond anything that they could stamp parts better and cheaper than anybody.

We did more than any of us ever expected. But what did we really gain...?

Mike's got "owner value" problems. His business is successful. He's more powerful and wealthier than he ever thought he would be. Yet, he's questioning all of it. *What did we really gain?*

If you're a business owner, you know Mike's not alone. For most business owners, no matter which generation of ownership they represent, success comes as a mixed blessing, all the good things combined with a surprising amount of "baggage."

Sure, we're not naive—we learn early there's no free lunch—but when success comes, it's always bigger and brassier and more costly than we figured. One minute we're putting out brush fires all over the landscape, and, suddenly, the next minute we're standing in a mature orchard with a hurricane predicted by morning.

We have time to see it coming, but we get blind-sided because of our natural focus. By experience, inclination, necessity, and just plain personality, business owners live in the short-term business reality. Immediate issues like cash flow needs, sudden opportunities, and annual profits, absorb most available waking hours—and a large portion of our dreams, as well.

Fortunately, it's possible to build a successful business this way. It happens all the time. Unfortunately, this focus on immediate business results is not the best way to build and maintain the owner value of that successful business over the long term.

Think about the impact of this "brush fire" outlook on just one key component of business value: management succession. Who would disagree that smooth ownership and management transition in a family business can enhance the value of that business, both to current owners and potential buyers? Yet, in companies mired in the immediate and the urgent, management transition is considered an "event" in some distant future and forever postponed: *"We'll get to that when the time comes."*

This is as sensible as storing the company's cash under a mattress. Companies don't suddenly *decide* to have a transition any more than a woman suddenly decides to give birth.

As long as transition is not planned or managed, life's surprising accidents have a high probability of turning into disasters. Like the worth of a house on a flood plain, the value of a business without a clear path to management transition is, by definition, depressed.

We can say the same thing about other value-enhancing steps like building strong management, for example, or developing a unified investment strategy for the business, even creating and maintaining a sound buy/sell agreement. Each can enhance the long-term value of the business.

In practice, building long-term owner value for owners of a successful business requires a dogged focus on the key components that support such value. The most important of these are:

1. Getting the right help

2. Putting the right people to work building that value (and paying them appropriately for doing so)

3. Managing agreement among the owners, especially on what they mean by "owner value."

Getting the Right Help

Convincing business-owner clients to install the engine — outside review — necessary to drive the management of owner value has probably been the toughest challenge I have faced as an advisor.

Back in 1981, Léon A. Danco and I wrote one of the first books on the concept of using outside directors in closely held businesses. Good book[1]. Great idea. The only problem was, most business owners didn't buy the concept.

Most business owners know the reasons:

- To preserve independence: *Why should I let someone tell me what to do?*

- To keep control: *Isn't that part of the attraction of being The Boss?*

- To avoid ill-informed advice: *What do outsiders (potential directors) know anyway?*

- To maintain confidentiality: *Why should I let outsiders know how things are run here?*

Certainly, there are some good reasons why we business owners prefer to keep things close to the chest, but the resulting hermetic seals of secrecy that encapsulate so many private companies can become silent killers. Instead of protecting successful businesses from outside interference, secrecy can doom them to atrophy, depriving them of the very dynamic flexibility that made them successful entrepreneurial ventures in the first place.

Today, many years since *Outside Directors in the Family-Owned Business* was published, it's apparent that most closely held companies aren't ready for a formal outside board.

This doesn't mean, however, that these businesses should proceed with no review at all. Success is just too big a deal for any of us to manage by ourselves. It simply means we must find more flexible and appropriate tools for bringing added skills and knowledge to the business. For this purpose, I, and a growing number of others, have found the use of advisory boards very effective and practical. (See *Chapter 4* for a detailed discussion of professional advisors and advisory boards.)

---

[1] Danco, Léon A. and Donald J. Jonovic, *Outside Directors in the Family-Owned Business: Why, When, Who, and How.* Cleveland: University Press, 1981.

BUILDING AN OWNER VALUE-DRIVEN MANAGEMENT TEAM

The quality and depth of management is the bedrock of owner value. Without an effective management team, the company's value to current owners or even a potential buyer is significantly decreased. On the other hand, a working, functioning team with a positive and identifiable impact on the bottom line can neutralize one of the most troubling negatives in the value of a closely held company—dependence on "The Boss(es)."

The effectiveness of the management team can be enhanced by identifying goals and establishing objectives. These are obvious value levers, yet they're too often missing from the toolbox of closely held companies.

To effectively manage a business as an investment, we must develop a formalized process of management performance evaluation— built on predefined responsibility definition, as well as objectives and measurements, which are both understood and agreed upon. Only then can the necessary credible measurement of performance, constructive critique, and formal review happen—along with a resulting compensation system which is real and fair.

Consider this thing called compensation. Whether it's an effective motivator is debatable, but, it can, in fact, be a useful and powerful tool for companies wishing to manage *value*. A well-planned and carefully structured compensation system, one which demonstrates a distinct connection between pay and results, can effectively focus management on increasing owner value. (See *Chapter 6* for detailed discussion of "strategic" approaches to compensation.)

Here's one of the many places where "outside review" is useful. Advisors can help business owners develop bonus systems clearly tied to performance (both the individual's and the company's). They can help explore options, including some form of equity bonus. Phantom stock plans, for example, while avoiding actual ownership participation, tie management effort to the bottom line and offer ownership-like rewards (see *Appendices 5* and *6*).

These are complex issues, but they *are* manageable—with the right help from the right people.

MANAGING THE "INVESTMENT STRATEGY"

Managing owner value in a closely held business must begin with defining a strategy for the investment, itself. Specifically, this requires, first, a formal process professionalizing the way the owners analyze, plan, communicate, and make decisions. This doesn't mean sending all our partners to leadership school or fitting them for three-piece suits. It means managing their roles and relationships so that they can work together productively, and make decisions *effectively*.

With the right process in place, it's possible to set an investment strategy, implement it productively, and monitor the impact of the business strategy on owner value.

All successful businesses go through this process in some way. Most founders and entrepreneurs tend to do it unconsciously. It becomes important to formalize the process when the founder's genius has produced significant growth, and the owner group begins to expand beyond one or two individuals.

You'll run into "process" throughout this book—not exactly a thrilling thought, I'm sure. Yet process is an absolutely essential tool, one we need to learn to use. Part of the reason we get blind-sided by our success is our lack of tools to manage the complexity that success brings.

Obviously, the key concept of "owner value" has as many definitions as there are owners. Internal communication must be structured to manage the effects of this richness of opinion.

In a closely held or family business, each owner can, and usually does, take a variety of roles: investor, director, manager, not to mention that unique role each plays as an individual. All these hats may not create identity crises, but when people speak to each other from different perspectives, communication pathways tend to get clogged. When the perspectives aren't defined and understood, confusion and conflict are almost inevitable.

For example, Brother Joe, half-owner and warehouse manager, wants to invest in increased warehouse space to improve order response time. He is thinking as a manager, and his "owner value" is defined as business growth. Brother Tom, half-owner and potential retiree, wants to improve his ROI by limiting capital improvements and increasing dividends. He is thinking as an investor, and his "owner value" translates to maximized personal cash flow.

Both of them are "right," yet their views are completely at odds! Little wonder business owners so often get stuck in holding patterns.

Managing how we "talk" to each other is essential to eliminating such potential deadlocks. Formalizing owner communication and decision-making is the focus of *Chapter 3*.

Communication isn't an end in itself, however. Not, at least, in a closely held business. We want our business communication to lead somewhere, to have a purpose. The flow diagram in *Figure I-1*, below, puts communication and decision making in the context of managing owner value.

In the simplest possible terms:

- The *owners* define an investment strategy (return on investment, growth rates, risk parameters, management philosophy — see *Chapter 5)*

- The *board* assures that the capital structure of the business makes sense, given the investment strategy (e.g., Should we be Sub-Chapter S?) and that the assets are managed through appropriate estate planning (see *Chapter 7)*

- The *board* also makes sure the investment strategy is translated into operating targets, and that management is appropriately organized and compensated (see *Chapter 6)* to meet those targets

- The *management team* creates and goes to work on a plan to meet their operational targets

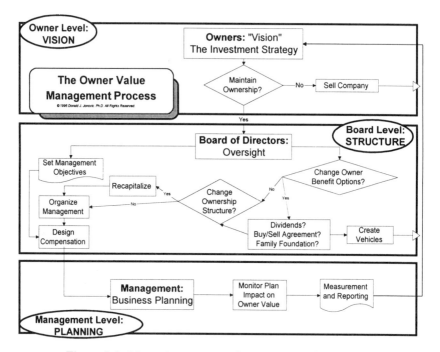

Figure I-1: *Managing owner value requires a formal process that begins with the definition of an investment strategy by the owners and "ends" with the evaluation of how well the business plan fulfills the investment goals the owners set. The process never really ends. Instead, it becomes a way of business life, a cycle that repeats itself at least annually.*

- The *owners*, the *board*, and *management* measure and monitor operational results (see, particularly, the discussion on advisors and boards in *Chapter 4*)

- The *owners* revisit and readjust the investment strategy (see *Chapter 3* on owner communication).

Owner value, through the investment strategy, is the driver throughout this process, and underlies decisions at all levels. The real purpose of the business is regularly defined, all activities are pointed at achieving that purpose, and the whole process is reviewed regularly for effectiveness.

We're talking here, not about revolution, but evolution—developing an overall professionalization around the concept of owner value. It's an ongoing process which requires a lot of time and effort. But given our real purpose, the building of value and opportunity for all the stakeholders in our business, the time and effort represent one of the most prudent investments we can make.

FOCUSING ON THE ULTIMATE LEGACY

Entrepreneurs and founders initially do a good job building business (and, thus, owner) value for themselves and their partners by combining talent and energy with the leverage of a short-term, reactive focus.

The more successful a business becomes, however, the less connected this operational myopia is to owner value. Threats loom ever greater, but farther in the future and harder to see. Solutions take more time to implement, and more time to show results. Internal skills and knowledge are engulfed by a rising tide of complexity. Internal confusion and conflict escalate. Value stagnates or drops, and our essential purpose, our reason for staying in business, declines with it.

This fundamental objective of business ownership is the preservation and building of owner value. It's true, different owners might define that value in different ways: using different combinations of career opportunity, cash flow, profits, equity, or market value. Equally true, this value can be harvested in many ways: through patient observation of growth, expanding career opportunity, frequent dividends, or even sale to a strategic buyer with investment of the proceeds in tax-free bonds.

However it's defined and distributed, though, owner value is only built and maintained through a value-management process. It's a process of regularly defining and reviewing owner objectives. It's a process of developing the ability to see and respond to distant threats. It's a means of ensuring that problem solving begins early and is relentlessly pursued. *It's a commitment to widening the base of knowledge and expertise available to the organization.*

Ultimately, value management is a commitment to linking the

owners, the organization, and the advisors together into a powerful "meta-management" that automatically scans in ever-widening circles for ways to protect and build owner value in the long term.

Before attempting to structure ourselves to manage owner value effectively, however, we first have to make sure we understand our history, so we won't be condemned to repeat it (*Chapter 1*), the owners, themselves (*Chapter 2*), and how we tend to trip up our own process of working together (*Chapter 3*).

YESTERDAY

1: The "Lessons" of History

"So, that's it, Frank. Our coverage ratio's gone to hell, and unless we take some action, we'll be out of cash and at the end of our credit line by June."

Frank sat still for a couple of minutes, studying the spreadsheets on the desk in front of him. He was stunned, yet somehow not really surprised by the CFO's bleak forecast.

When he accepted the VP-Marketing job at Halstead Industries, Mark and Marvin Halstead, the owners, told him there were problems in some of the other divisions and subsidiaries. But, now, almost a year after taking the job, he was getting his first look at overall corporate finances, behind the barn, so to speak, from a guilty and hesitant CFO.

"You're sticking your neck out showing me all this, aren't you, Vince?"

"I suppose," the Chief Financial Officer replied, shrugging with resignation. "But I had to do something to get some action. The Halsteads are always strictly need-to-know. I have no problem with that, except they don't understand how much their people actually need to know."

Frank stood and walked to the window. He watched a huge crane lower another beam into the shell of the new warehouse.

"So," he said, finally turning to face Vince, "you need me to help you convince Marv and Mark we have to sell off the vacuum forming business, and base that recommendation on information I'm not supposed to have."

"That's about the size of it," Vince agreed.

"Well," Frank said, taking his chair and pulling the papers toward him, "let's see how the uninformed go about performing

the unlikely.
"What a hell of a way to run a railroad..."

If there is one characteristic that best denotes most business owners and most closely held businesses, it's secrecy. Sensitive (and many times not so sensitive, but relatively important) information is kept from suppliers, competitors, regulators, friends, relatives, and, as Vince, the CFO knew, even from the insiders.

Closely held businesses are not properly named. To be accurately described, they should be called *hermetically sealed businesses*. This trait, more than most other cultural characteristics common in private businesses, is a root cause of destroyed owner value.

To understand *that*, we have to review a little history.

THE "HERMETIC SEAL:" HOW SECRECY EVOLVES — AND KILLS

Business ownership means waking up unemployed every morning.

To endure that each day, keeping your digestion somewhat intact, you gotta be tough. Owning your own business often means lying in bed in the middle of the night, wide awake, in one of those perennial 3:00 a.m. "blink" sessions, staring at the crack in the bedroom ceiling and wondering how you'll survive the current crisis, whatever it happens to be.

Competition is the driver. That's one of the fundamentals of being in business, and what makes capitalism so great. What they don't tell you in business school, though, is that the competition we face is not limited to the other people who make or deliver our product. Today's competitive climate carries added dimensions in the form of all kinds of opposition, like life and death struggles with major suppliers, with the government, with partners, fellow shareholders, even family.

In the early years, founding entrepreneurs face opposition

from nattering critics and all-knowing second-guessers. "How can you do that?" "It'll never work." "What you really need is a business plan." Well-intentioned suggestions? Perhaps. But most are worth less than the amount paid for such "advice." It's bad enough starting a business against the clean (and sometimes less-than-clean) competition in the marketplace. What's worse is climbing that slippery mountain with a crowd of nay-saying onion-breathers trying to convince you it can't be done.

Well, it *can* be done! You simply know it. The best strategy in the face of all that carping? Obviously, keep quiet. Tough it out alone.

Doubts? Sure, but when they come up, *crush 'em.* Mistakes? Lots of 'em. Best to learn from them, bury them and move along. Disasters? Far too many, but, whatever happens, don't let any of *them* know. Don't give *them* the satisfaction. Don't fan their flames of doubt.

Eventually, there are triumphs. Victory! When it works, it's a high like standing at the Matterhorn's summit, surveying all the world below. Usually, for most entrepreneurs it's a solitary high. Typically, few others really helped. Most, as we've seen, muttered doubts, and some even shoved roadblocks in our path.

So we're tough in defeat. We're stalwart in victory.

And, either way, because of how it happened, we wind up very much the lone cats in the jungle.

Tigers roam their jungles, stealthily, secretly. They pad quietly through the undergrowth. They drag their prey to private places, and they bury their droppings. When they roar, it's more to intimidate than to communicate.

Secrecy. It's our armor. We have it like turtles have shells, and we carry it with us wherever we go. We justify it in many ways, but few of our explanations and protestations come close to the *real* reasons for our secrecy.

Hiding Trouble in the Bad Times

The truth is that sometimes, especially in the beginning, we need to hide how bad things are. Those are the times when there's no money in the till. No cash in petty cash. No balance in the balance sheet. No income in the income statement. No "P" in the P&L.

We can't let the bank know, because first thing they'll do is call the loan. If the suppliers find out, they'll put us on C.O.D. The employees might panic and quit. Our in-laws might laugh, or worse talk about us pityingly when our backs are turned.

Nobody needs to know the trouble we see. We can handle it, all of it. Male or female, we lie in our beds, tense and wide awake in our "blink" sessions, bathed in sweat, worrying about how to survive the most recent crisis. There's no loneliness like lying in that pool of damp perspiration, desperately clinging to the remains of our enthusiasm and summoning enough strength to get through the night and enough guts to face the next day.

These are the beginnings of the hermetic seal, those nights when only obstinate tunnel vision gets us through. Here, the seeds are planted for distrust of outsiders. Here, also, begin the fierce loyalties toward those who stood by us in adversity — that early key employee, the banker who ignored the facts and loaned us money anyway.

In the tough times (which can occur at any time in the business life cycle) secrecy makes some real sense. It may even be essential to continued survival. But this doesn't explain the CIA approach to information that tends to pervade and endure in our businesses long *after* they've become successful. With success, a whole different class of excuses for secrecy emerges.

Hiding Success in the Good Times

As business, revenues, cash flow and profits grow, new reasons emerge for keeping things close to the chest. Mostly, we discover that there are many realities about our fiscal policies and results that most people just wouldn't understand.

Friends, in some cases even good ones, tend to become uncomfortable with us if our income levels grow out of synch with theirs. What we take for granted as a life style suddenly outstrips what used to be shared tastes and preferences. Because we value the people we love and respect, the obvious answer is to keep quiet about our success. *Don't make a big thing about it and maybe nobody'll notice.*

But keeping friends and some stability in our social life isn't the only reason we stay secretive. Take employees, for example. They always seem to have a mistaken notion about how much money a business can generate, and they have almost no notion of the level of risk we bear. If they saw the net income, that misunderstanding could turn directly to resentment, dissatisfaction and, ultimately, unreasonable demands for increased compensation.

Solution? Simple. Just don't show them the numbers — the same conclusion that Mark and Marv Halstead came to in the epigram that opened this chapter.

Finally, there is that little acknowledged fact of business ownership that "profit" is a bad thing. We really don't want to make a profit, and we often do everything possible to avoid it. What we *do* want, really, is to *break even*, at a higher level every fiscal year.

I've seen estimates that roughly $300 billion is consumed annually in the United States to support the tax compliance (or more accurately for a for-profit business, tax *avoidance*) infrastructure. That's about equal to one year's national economic growth. Based on the fact that private businesses account for a majority of the growth in our economy, we wouldn't be too far off concluding they pay a large share of that compliance cost. That's a lot of energy and time spent breakin' even.

We all hate paying taxes, but should tax avoidance (and the secrecy it requires) be the primary focus of our management, accounting, and planning?

Secrecy's Main Tool: "Creative Accounting"

Closely held businesses have developed some of the most creative accounting systems ever seen. They follow all the basic rules. All the relevant events are reported. It's all there.

Just try to *find* it.

I remember many times sitting in early meetings of new boards, going over what appeared to be disappointing budget-to-actual results, which, after painful discussion, turned out to be results of *ad hoc* decisions by managers whether to capitalize or expense a large outlay. If you peel back the polished *Times New Roman* veneer of the accounting statement, you'll find all sorts of "interpretations" underneath. In the Byzantine bowels of family business ledgers we find arcane oddities like "shareholder override expense" to cover life insurance funding cross-purchase agreements. There are interpretive twists, too, like the "corporate" aircraft on the books of a company doing business in a 50-mile radius.

Most of this *mazeophilia* is driven by common sense decisions to minimize tax exposure (it's all a matter of interpretation). The net result, however, is to dim the lights in the Accounting Department so low that even the Controller can lose sight of what's going on.

For the entrepreneur, and even for the business in difficulty, this secrecy is understandable and, sometime, appropriate. The trouble is, once secrecy takes root in the closely held business culture, it grows like kudzu, inexorably burying the facts — the information required to make sound business decisions about growth and about the future. Ultimately, what's buried is the opportunity the future could hold.

Because of this hermetic seal that almost naturally encases the successful privately held business, it is very difficult for owners to figure out the nature and performance of their investment. Instead of evolving into a science, management increasingly degrades into alchemy. Advisors, stumbling through this fog, understandably throw up their hands in hopeless confusion.

Building a successful business and long-term owner value under these conditions is like climbing a mountain wearing blinders and floppy sandals.

Thus, you will find a lot of attention in this book focused on *information:* how to clean it up, make it accurate, make it accessible, and make it useful. Until we are able, as business owners, to make clear, honest numbers available to ourselves, our directors, our managers and our advisors, we will fail to achieve the potential of the businesses we own.

We may fail, in the end, even to *keep* those businesses we have guarded so closely. But there is hope and there are answers to battling this silent enemy of success.

Secrecy can be slow poison, but there are antidotes. (See *Chapter 4* on opening up to advisors, and *Chapter 6* on compensating management for building owner value.)

MAZES OF LOVE AND AUTHORITY: HOW HISTORY "DESIGNS" THE PROBLEM

Every business has a founder. It can be a single entrepreneur, a few siblings, some non-related partners, even other partnerships or corporations. Whoever or whatever is behind the conception, the same evolution usually follows the birth.

The consequence of the long series of middle-of-the night "blink" sessions is secrecy, as I've said, as well as an institutionalized "Horatio at the Bridge" mentality: it's us against the tax man, the competition, the suppliers, the employees, sometimes even the customers. The result, often, is an increasingly distant relationship between the owner-manager(s)/shareholders and most others who relate to the business, particularly the employees.

Nobody Cares for It Like We Do

It's not a distance of exploitation. Business owners generally take very seriously their responsibility to treat employees fairly. Rather, it's a distance of confidence, somewhat of a lack of trust, translated frequently into questions like: "Why can't our employees care about this business the way we do?"

The Accounting Department is, in many respects, at the core of the problem. No matter what stage in its evolution (it typically begins as a checkbook, eventually becomes "Bookkeeping," then evolves through a Controller's Office, to ultimately reside in the person of a Chief Financial Officer), "Finance" acquires and keeps, at the behest of the business owner(s), one principal and overriding function: that of the Financial Dragon.

The role of "Finance" in the closely held business is to hover like the fierce, scaled beasts of mythology over the family jewels, belching foul gases on any of the non-initiated (read: non-owners) who dare to venture near or ask probing questions.

This combination of an anemic confidence in employees with a secrecy-driven, institutionalized lack of objective financial measurement cripples the process of delegation. As the closely held business grows, more people are added to handle the exploding amount of work, but they are kept on a relatively short rein, focused more on tactical errands than on strategic projects. All the while, the owner-managers become more and more burdened with (read: *buried in*) detail.

If we draw an organization chart of the typical successful closely held business, we end up either with the sanitized "public relations" version (the one that shows up in the local business weekly and has no correlation with the reality of the situation), or we have a convoluted web of interweaving lines of authority that, seen from any distance, looks more like an explosion in a spaghetti factory than a workable business operation.

Nepotism: When Employment Is Relative

Add to this what is perhaps the most important "wrinkle" unique to the closely held company: nepotism. Unlike, say, IBM, where children of shareholders have no special claim as potential employees, closely held companies face the challenge of managing that embarrassment of wealth called the owners' offspring and relatives. They can be real assets to the business. They can be dangerous liabilities. Most often, they're a raw material with low definition and high potential impact.

Relatives, offspring, and in-laws tend to adhere to the organization at all sorts of odd angles and configurations. In first and second-generation businesses, the company is almost like another room in the house. People grow up in it. They play around it, hide in the corners, fight in the hallways. Working there is often "something we've always done." Employment has more to do with puberty than with any defined needs of the organization. Later, in those businesses which survive into future generations, politics, family logrolling, peacekeeping, and loyalty replace the endocrine system as drivers of the nepotism process.

Now, I'm not saying that nepotism is inherently evil, or that the beneficiaries of the preference are necessarily incompetent, corrupt, or inept. Often, in fact, those who survive such a misguided and destructive process prove to have mettle far beyond the ordinary.

No, the key danger of nepotism (and why it has such a bad name in history) is that it seldom takes the needs of the *organization* into account when the organization is being structured. Instead, individual and/or family needs come first.

One of the principal reasons owners struggle to keep a business private is the fact that it can provide opportunity for the next generation. While this certainly increases the value of the business to the owning families, it can have the entirely opposite effect on owner value in the future. Nepotism is essentially a concern with the "immediate legacy," which can sharply distract ownership, board, and management from the *ultimate* legacy: long-term owner value.

Recognizing this, the owners, managers, and advisors can work together toward qualified family management. Nepotism's benefits can, in fact, be reaped without the associated evils if effective processes for qualifying successor management and slotting the *right* person in the *right* job for the *right* reason are in place. (See *Chapters 6 and 9.)*

In every closely held business that's more than one generation old, history, in a sense, is a partner and those who don't understand history are condemned to repeat it. Another uncomfortable fate awaits

11

those who attempt to understand the present without understanding the people who inhabit it.

People, therefore, are the next issue to consider.

2: The Players

The meeting was showing no signs of running down. Jack glanced surreptitiously at his watch and wondered, again, if the battery had died.

One of the outside directors was droning on about coming changes in the supplier relationship. Everybody else listened politely (and, Jack thought, a little vacantly) to these observations they'd all heard from him before at prior meetings.

Jack's eyes stopped at the head of the table, on the familiar face of his father-in-law. Joe gave every appearance of rapt attention to the director's words, the warmth in his eyes reflecting the long years of friendship between the two industry statesmen.

Respect for Joe was universal throughout the company, and he had earned the same from just about everybody in the industry as well. From the day he founded the company, 38 years before, to this moment, when he presided over a $150 million international manufacturing company, his guidance had been firm and visionary.

Well, Jack reminded himself, not *quite* to this moment. Those so-called "changes" were actually world-shattering revolutions. Joe simply didn't see it. One of the builders in his field, he was now blinded to changes in his own industry which were as obvious as the rising sun.

Why I left IBM to work for Joe I'll never know, Jack thought glumly. He brought more outside experience than anyone else in the company, yet Joe simply thought of him as a "corporate type," who didn't understand the nature of entrepreneurship. Whenever Jack tried to discuss what he saw as a potential strategic threat, Joe would smile patiently and tell him he needed

more time in the industry to get a better perspective. *You worry too much, Jack,* Joe would advise him.
And you, Old Man, don't worry enough!

Jack and Joe each have a business "vision." So do the directors in that room. Same company. Same facts. Very different conclusions.

We *all* have a vision. The very role of intelligence, in fact, is to construct a meaningful reality (i.e., vision) out of the bloomin' confusion that surrounds us. To make sense of things, and to be able to act effectively, we build frameworks in which to fit the important facts, which we also carefully select for "relevance."

It's an obvious, but little considered fact that we are all separated from the outside world by a wall of flesh. Years ago, my doctoral research focused on the process of converting raw sense data — light waves, pressures, molecular shapes — into such brilliant results as Picasso paintings and Cole Porter compositions.

If each of us constructs his realities out of raw sense data, I reasoned (as had many others before me), to communicate effectively, we each need an accurate understanding of each others' *reality*.

Complete understanding of another's reality is impossible, of course, but it is possible to discern general outlines, certain color schemes, overall themes in the way others approach the world. If we could achieve this sort of outline understanding, we could increase the probability that any discussion about decisions we needed to make jointly will bear fruit.

This isn't just theoretical psychology. It's a prescription for communication that can be very effective in developing agreement. While this understanding may never be complete, we can make a significant start.

In working with clients, then, I generally start from basic templates developed over many years spent working with successful people, who, despite their unique personalities, tend to share some consistent outlooks, based upon the role they play.

What follows are my personal working "templates." Inevitably, we each have our own, but these might help you refine yours:

THE BOSS(ES): *I* RUN THE SHOW...

We begin with "The Boss" for obvious reasons.

Few men or women — maybe Federal judges on the bench, captains of ships at sea in wartime, but few others — possess the kind of power the business owner earns and eventually takes for granted.

Armed with a power of control, or "The Vote," in the case of significant minority owners in multi-partner businesses, business owners hold in their hands a ring of keys to the kingdom. They have legal access to the confidential financial data. They can push business and personal agendas with some considerable influence. They can make decisions based on their own criteria and, generally, not have to explain those criteria or even justify them to nattering critics or sideline quarterbacks.

Owners are deferred to by non-owners. The bigger the business and the more wealth involved, the more this is true. They are courted by suppliers, solicited by consultants and advisors.

They are cultivated by non-owner employees. They are treated with deference, if not respect, by fellow owners or partners, all of whom prefer to operate by consensus and, therefore, avoid outright conflict or disagreement.

Owners are feted at Rotary meetings. They are offered leadership roles in trade associations. They are invited to serve on civic boards and are targets for "development" people looking to build boards of trustees.

All of this is natural. Such leadership, influence, and respect are some of the driving forces of western society and real sources of satisfaction for active and involved people.

This adulation can become destructive, however, when the

owner begins to confuse this respect for something like omniscience.

The Founders

For the lone founder/entrepreneur, this respect, power and influence is well-nigh absolute — which, usually, is a good thing for the new business, because few new ventures could survive the confusion and waffling of a founding by committee.

Founders, generally, *do* run the show, and they run it very well, thank you. Their reality is formed around two simple, empirical facts: that nobody cares about their business the way they do, and that there are no free lunches. Anyone who hasn't "done it" themselves, and who disagrees with these truths, is suspect.

Successful business founders are geniuses, entrepreneurial virtuosos with an inbred artistry that allows them to juggle people, machines, markets, competitors, and customers into a stunning blur of profitable synergy. They run their businesses the way NASCAR drivers guide their machines, with an unconscious deftness drawn from technical understanding, superb reflexes, and superhuman vision.

How did I know exactly when to pass that guy ahead? I can't say. I just did it when it felt right. What's the difference? It worked, and that's what counts isn't it?

It's easy to question and carp from the pits, the founder thinks. But until you've spent the years I have hugging the groove, you'll never have the *feel, that survival instinct.*

As Joe in the opening epigram to this chapter said to his son-in-law: *You worry too much, Jack...*

The Founders' Heirs

In subsequent generations, particularly when little remains of the founder but an oil painting, this absolute power tends to dissipate somewhat, as ownership flows like sap along expanding "stirpes" or branches of descent from the original business pioneer(s).

Still, even with dispersed ownership, the sense of being anointed lingers among shareholders. In multi-owner businesses, instead of an entrepreneur holding court in an office full of hard-won memorabilia and photos with the famous, power is exercised from "board rooms," co-presidencies, or "executive committees."

These multi-owner councils are made up of people acutely aware of their twin burdens of business ownership and management responsibility. They attend meetings as a matter of both duty and right, to exercise oversight on issues ranging from the long-range strategy of the business to the color of the labels on the shrink-wrapped package.

At stake for second-generation owners is nothing less than the survival of the entrepreneurial vision of the founder(s). They have their feet planted in two very different worlds: the history that bred success, and the future that builds on, harvests, and, potentially, *threatens* that success.

Their challenge is to stay upright as those two worlds continually diverge, swaying precariously, one foot on a pier, the other in a tossing boat.

In the second ownership generation, the founding King Arthur has vanished into the lake and the Roundtable of Heirs now governs the kingdom. Their duty is clear.

The strategy for success, however, is not clear at all. The evident genius of the founder(s), usually deeply respected by all, functions less and less effectively as a guide. Ultimately, the Old King's ways become less relevant, less in tune with the marketplace. The battlements remain manned and the swords are kept sharp. The only trouble is, outside the walls of Camelot the world has discovered gunpowder!

Compared to the founders, second-generation owners are more likely to see value in outsiders, strangers — but not all that *much* more. Steeped in the training of the secretive founders, they, too, are hesitant, careful. They are secretive, still, but their genius is a recognition

17

that, important as brains are to success, the key to the future is in the detail of *implementation.*

People from outside (either the business or the ownership group) are no longer suspect *on their face.* The insiders just don't know how to select them, use them, inform them, and/or trust them. But they do need help, and they know it.

As a group, founders' heirs are not as homogenous as were their forebears. Founders, no matter what their social, economic, or financial background, tend to be mavericks at heart. Their heirs, some of them, can be mavericks, too, but that's not a requirement of survival as it was with the founder. Depending on upbringing, background, and genetics, heirs to founders are more likely than their predecessors to reflect the distribution of personality in the general population, as a class.

They see the business, not as a dream to be achieved, but as a tool to be *used.* They have much to gain with success, true, but also a lot to lose. Also, they are seldom operating alone, given the rarity of only children having only children. They have "partners," some of whom are like them, usually more of whom are as different as can be.

Thus, the second generation adds a new strategic variable to the business: internal conflict. One of the second-generation's greatest strategic challenges is to manage inherent differences and balance competing strengths so that they add to the business rather than paralyze and destroy it.

The Third-Generation (and After) Owners

In the third generation and beyond, the Roundtable becomes a Parliament. Arthur's legend (i.e., the business history and values) is all but forgotten. If the old swords still exist, they no longer inspire confidence in the users. The grandchildren, in short, barely knew their grandparents — in terms of business, at least.

The new owners want very much to step into the shoes of the second-generation old knights, but they know less of actual battle. They have been apprentices in many guilds (the summer job is really an "exposure" program), but haven't fought any important battles. They haven't been tested under fire. They work diligently to learn and to be recognized, but seldom know what it takes to be considered a player.

They look at each other and wonder about many things, including who will progress faster than I, under what circumstances, and will I be able to live with the result? In fact, it's not even a real competition. Generally, they don't know each other well, having been raised in different families, under different rules.

Grandchildren of founders (and beyond) are as likely as anyone else to be skilled and capable. They want to preserve The Dream that drove their forebears, but, in the confusion of change and complexity, they aren't quite sure what that "Dream" is, much less how to preserve it. They surely are confused, increasingly, about who should or can make it all happen.

So, these are the owners. Whatever their stresses and confusions, they do, by definition and legal right, of whatever generation they might be, run the show. Or do they?

Maybe we would do well to check with the others involved—right after we've summarized a few key realities and implications of business ownership:

Key Realities for Owners

- Business ownership provides one of the few guarantees of power, respect and influence in life.

- Business ownership, like royalty, tends to be a lonely experience, even in the midst of many people.

- Partnerships (including multiple shareholders of corporations) are difficult and stressful.

Implications

- *Business owners should give priority to realistic self-evaluation and listening to others.* Because the power

19

of ownership is real and significant, it can not only isolate but *corrupt* the holder of that power. As the slave would whisper in the ear of the victorious Roman general as he paraded through the streets of the ancient capital: *"Remember, you are only a mortal."*

- *Secrecy in the organization should be regularly examined and questioned.* Too often, the stated reasons for keeping important and essential information close to the chest (e.g., competitors might use it, the employees would want a raise) are only masks for wanting to keep absolute control and the fear of losing it.

- *Managing the way we connect multiple shareholders into an effective team is a strategic necessity.* Buy/Sell agreements, objective compensation systems, owner vision, formal channels of communication, all are tools for making sure businesses aren't torn apart by owner conflict from within.

The Spouse(s): You *Think* You Do!

In this business drama we're defining, as in most dramas, the key players are usually part of a couple. Successors/heirs come as couples. Key employees have spouses. Owners do, too.

So what's the big revelation, one might ask?

It's not simply the existence of spouses; that's too obvious. The big surprise to most people is that spouses of owners are generally the most unrepresented (and unrecognized) people of power in the organization.

Those owners, today, who were born before World War II, put it most directly: *"My wife/husband is not involved in the business."*

Partners (especially in that age group) are less subtle: *"Our spouses have never been involved in the business, and that is one of the primary reasons we've all gotten along all these years."*

Younger business-owning couples — baby-boomers and later — may not have quite the same comfortable insulation between business and married life as do their older peers who, almost by definition, keep their spouses in a profound state of darkness. As the ownership diversifies over the generations, however, a certain presumption grows almost naturally that the only good partner's spouse is an *invisible* partner's spouse.

Anyone who assumes that "out of sight" means "out of action" when it comes to owners' spouses, however, makes an unrealistic assumption and a potentially fatal mistake. These spouses may not spend a lot of time around the business, but their lives are steeped in its pressures and benefits.

They are *partners* to their owner-spouses, actually. They lie in bed next to them at night, during those "blink" sessions, listening to the owner's perspiration hissing like Niagara Falls over the horizon.

Spouses have their own careers, either in business, the professions, or homemaking, and they surely have their own worries, but they know that whatever is eating at the strong, silent entrepreneur next to them is eventually going to mean trouble. Trouble for the owner's spouse comes in many forms. It can be financial ruin (or, more likely, the periodic or sometimes chronic cash drought). It can involve the kids, particularly those working in the business, who may be looking for an ally and advocate to help them overthrow, disarm or at least influence the current owners. It can lurk around the back door as an ongoing dispute among partners, discoloring business, family, social and all other aspects of life.

An owner's spouse's trouble can also come as justifiable worries about a loved one who works too hard, too long, under too much stress. It can come in the guise of retirement plans that have about as much reality as a Tolkien fantasy, or as much possibility as a Star Trek adventure, but seem, nevertheless, to be driving the future into some very undesirable directions.

I can see it now, the spouse thinks in the charged darkness, *he'll be down there in the kitchen at 5:30 in the morning someday. I'll go down and urge him to come back to bed because he's retired and he can sleep in. Instead, he'll wave me in, sit me down and ask why, all these years, I've put up with the dishwasher located on the wall furthest from the cabinet holding the pots and pans.*

What will I do? He'll drive me crazy!

Spouses of owners may be ministers without portfolio, but they have a deep and abiding interest in the progress of the business and the people who own it. Their reality is defined by a lack of direct control and influence, which forces them to apply indirect control, either through subtle diplomacy or not-so-subtle hostility and threat.

However the pressure is brought to bear on "The Boss(es)," because the owner and spouse share such an intimate and influential relationship, that pressure can move mountains of deep-rooted granite.

It's not unusual, for example, for business owners or partners to meet on a controversial issue, come to what appears to be consensus, yet discover the next morning that one of them has changed his or her mind. Reflection? Second thoughts? Possibly. Spousal input at the end of the day? Probably.

Non-involved owners' spouses do not share the emotional commitment owners have to their businesses. They may share it to some extent, but seldom do they adopt the single-minded focus that comes with being steeped in a business. Spouses are more objective. They tend to see the business more in terms of cost/benefit equations than market or career opportunity, or ego booster/breaker.

Assuming they are not involved day-to-day, whatever reward they get from "operations" is strictly monetary, in the form of salary, bonus, and dividends. Consequently, what they "pay" for that reward leads them to look at the business more coldly than do their spouses.

They pay, not in job stress, but in *emotional* stress as their spouses come home distracted, exhausted, cranky, frustrated, and maybe even angered at their business partners. They pay as they see their financial security threatened by inaction, indecisiveness, conflict, or just plain "hair-brained schemes."

They pay in the form of watching the relationship between their spouse and their children take a back seat to the business. They pay through their children, whose futures become inextricably entwined with a business ill-prepared and unlikely to let them grow to their full potential.

These prices aren't always exacted, of course. Sometimes the business brings opportunity, joy, and fulfillment.

Sometimes.

Spouses of owners have their own "strategic" view of the business. That view, however, is seldom considered or taken seriously in any public discussion of the business.

In the background, though, that view is advanced and acknowledged in many ways. And, in many ways, it can be as valuable and important to the survival of the organization as that of the people who supposedly "run the show."

Key Realities for the Owners' Spouses

- The business is critically important in the life of the owner's spouse. Owners' spouses are deeply involved in the business, whether or not they work within it or are informed as to what is going on.

- Spouses are key contributors to the success or failure of the business, whether or not they draw a salary.

Implications

- *Keep owners' spouses informed.* Consider owners' and partners' spouses as, themselves, owners. Respect and communicate with them accordingly. Remember: a key concept in successful sales is to ensure that you reach *all* key decision makers.

- *The business contribution of an owner's spouse must be appropriately rewarded.* This can range anywhere from a regular "thank you" (through word and deed) for absorbing a domestic/child rearing role, all the way through phantom stock ownership (e.g., for spouses in the business) to actual stock ownership for spouses in return for the positive difference they make.

THE SUCCESSOR(S): I *WILL* RUN THE SHOW...

The adjective that best describes the majority of owners' offspring who work in the closely held or family business is "frustrated."

The frustration has many sources, ranging from getting no respect as green neophytes in make-work jobs to spending 15 years in the under-rewarded service of the current owner, marking time based on vague promises.

These aren't key employees, remember. These are young (at least younger than the current owners) men and women who, regardless of experience or competence, hold their jobs *principally* because they are related in some way to the current owners of the business.

For successors, the job isn't simply a career. There's a dream attached to that job, a fuzzy promise, a picture of "someday, this will be mine."

Early Management Education

The business has usually been a lifelong influence, starting out as a playground where the very young son or daughter goes into work with Dad or Mom to jam copiers, erase hard disks, and leave trucks out of gear while the adults are buried in their offices.

"Go do something and let me work for a while."

Business education for the business heir usually begins on the fringes of dawning consciousness, watching Dad or Mom sit ex-

24

hausted in a favorite chair, mumbling barely understood complaints.

Something called *"OH-shuh"* is on our backs. The bank is threatening to call something and the employees are ungrateful. Taxes are eating us alive. It's a lousy industry. Uncle Charlie is a boob.

And Daddy or Mommy keeps saying someday this'll all be *mine*!?

The Summer Job

Later, the business becomes a sort of summer home, the obvious and tax-wise way to fill the out-of-school-with-nothing-to-do months. It provides a place that the "privileged" immature can make mistakes in full view of increasingly unimpressed future subordinates. This is the "summer job," a perennial tradition among families who own businesses, whatever the particular generation of ownership.

Some of these jobs are real. A few of them can actually be good and valuable experiences. Most, on the other hand, involve work one couldn't easily force a chain gang to do. In almost all cases, these summer jobs are principally designed to provide a deductible allowance for the son, daughter, nephew, niece, or whomever.

Kids are kids. Some love to work. Some would rather be anywhere else than punching a time clock in the family business. On paper routes or flipping burgers somewhere else, it's possible to work out that difficult connection between hard work and life's desires without anyone else's opinions and judgments becoming long-term baggage.

It makes a LARGE difference whether the speaker of the words below is a family member or not:

"I had a couple beers before coming into work and accidentally dumped that whole vat of boiling fat into the frozen meat locker. Boy, my boss about had an aneurysm right there on the spot."

"I wonder what ever happened to him."

If the heir worked outside the business, it doesn't really matter what happened to him in the summer employment of his youth. One the other hand, if that "job" was in the family's business, that onetime "boss" now works for the kid, which certainly doesn't keep him from telling that story and other embarrassing peccadilloes to anyone who's willing to listen. Since the stories concern the Boss's kid, that means just about everybody.

Should He/She Work Elsewhere First?

In *Appendix A-2* you can see a sample family employment policy. Consider one of the key provisions written there:

> Entry-level employment of family members is discouraged.

This is a policy prescribed by many specialists in transition of family and closely held businesses. It's a wisdom based on the presumption that outside experience before settling into the family company is valuable for both the successor and the business.

It does *not,* however, reflect how things tend to go in the real world. More often than not, heirs to business owners move directly from school (and the summer job/deductible allowance) into jobs in the family's company. They become "Management Trainees."

This happens for a lot of reasons, most of them unrelated to actual business needs. More likely, the employment is driven by such factors as the heir's total commitment to a career in the business or the lack of realistic employment alternatives.

The problem is not so much that the family business is a bad environment or, somehow, unsuitable. The problem is one of timing and definition. The *timing* is seldom related to company needs. It's more likely to be related to points in the heir's life cycle (graduation, marriage and "settling down," etc.). This usually leads to the problem of *definition:* "if there were a real job available, we would've filled it when it opened with someone who was qualified for the job."

The dilemma: The heir is "ready" for employment in the company, but the company has no immediate need (real job) for the heir. The usual solution: The heir gets hired anyway and comes in to an ill-defined trainee role, where jobs are made for the heir on an *ad hoc* basis as he or she moves from department to department "learning the ropes."

Although, as I've said, such nepotism is not an *inherently* evil practice, there are real and serious negatives at work here.

First, it is a career path not available to others, which indicates favoritism, thereby putting all kinds of pressure, spotlights and undesirable attention on the successor trainee.

Further, without real job definition (real goals and actual measures of success), the process does little to give the successor a sense of his or her own accomplishment or self-worth. Finally, with no future-directed plan, how much of value is being taught?

Exactly what does this "management trainee" learn? History, mostly. The training usually centers around *our* "culture," *our* "policies," *our* "customers," *our* way of doing things. As a management trainee, a successor basically learns how to run yesterday's business in an environment where it is almost impossible to develop any real and lasting credibility as a competent manager.

There is a large set of reasons why heirs to family or closely held company ownership should work elsewhere before joining their own business. Two major reasons are that working elsewhere is much more likely to develop credibility and self-confidence. A third, as I've mentioned, is the chance to make early mistakes with people you'll never see again.

The human animal responds to pressure, challenge, adventure, the unfamiliar. If each of us is honest, looking into our past, we see that the times we learned the most were usually times we were the most out of our element and depending upon our wits or responding to the rigorous demands of a respected and objective authority.

Our literature is filled with adventure stories. We are fascinated by explorers and pioneers. Entrepreneurs, by definition, are pioneers; they feed on risk and thrive on adventure. Yet they tend, in their success, to try to protect their descendants from the very stresses that made the entrepreneurs successful.

Exposure. Adventure. Risk. Challenge. If we are planning a training program for the next generation, these should be the touchstones of whether the program is meaningful, or merely a comfortably paved path leading to nowhere but frustration and dissatisfaction.

The "Crown Prince(ss)"

"Management Trainees" eventually graduate and become "managers." One would hope the transition would occur because the individual involved actually qualified for more responsibility. In practice, however, it more likely occurs because of family and/or economic pressure (e.g., demands by the disgruntled successor, unceasing intercession by the successor's determined but not-involved-in-the-business other parent, or a potential revolution fomented by the successor's even more disgruntled spouse).

When working with family successors, I'm frequently reminded of the disgusting old locker room witticism that you know your socks need laundering when you throw them against the wall and they stick. In many ways, this is analogous to the way "real" jobs are found for heirs of owners.

As before, if there were a real job available, it would probably have been filled long before by someone qualified. When the heir enters the company's management ranks because of non-business reasons (the usual situation), a hole isn't being filled. It's being *dug*. The heir is thrown at the organization chart, so to speak, and where he or she sticks is where he or she stays.

The heir goes from being a management migrant (the department-of-the-week training program) to an "assistant-to" (generally known as a "Vice President of..."). Since the job was "made," the responsibility coming with it is ill-defined and variable. It is usually determined and re-determined by such "impartial" and "objective" people as a senior family member or even the heir's own parent.

Although such a system is undesirable, it can work, and sometimes does. The probability is high, though, that this undefined situation can last for many years. The owners, senior in age and perspective, believe in being thorough. They take the long view on qualification, and prefer that the successor-heir get more experience. They can afford the long view. After all, they're in the prime of life. There's plenty of time...

The heir, on the other hand, sees time slipping away. The older generation, to the heir's thinking, is obviously past its prime, and, concluding this, the young successor resolves not to waste his best years.

This view is not all wrong. In reality, spending years in a successor role *can* mean wasting precious years. Men and women in their late 30s and early 40s generally become less employable elsewhere with every passing year. Add to that uncomfortable fact the realization that the years spent in the family business job amount more to "helping out" than building any sort of résumé others would understand or value, and we shouldn't be shocked that the successors become increasingly panicked and revolutionary.

It's critical to understand the claustrophobia that can mark the experience of business owners' successors. They toil away, day after day, in ignorance of their real responsibility, the objectives they're supposed to meet, the career path ahead, and even the long-range plan for the business and its ownership. When they complain or question the situation, they're generally counseled to be patient.

Be patient? Right. For all I know, Dad, or Uncle Charlie, or whoever holds the gold, will die tomorrow, throwing it all to Uncle Sam, or the Courts, or, worse, my cousins. If I get 'em mad, they could even sell the place out from under me.

Still, because of family, love, the remains of trust, and the still-clinging hope of having it all, successor-heirs often are willing to wait for that distant "blessed event," when someday…it'll all be theirs.

They may be willing, but their spouses are a different story altogether.

Key Realities for the Successors

- Successors have a scarlet "S" emblazoned on their foreheads, and it keeps them in an unrelenting and unforgiving spotlight.

- Successors, of all the managers in the business, have the greatest need for job definition, clear objectives, and objective review. They are also the least likely to have the benefit of any of these.

Implications

- *Discourage entry-level career positions for owners' children in the company.*

- *Encourage initial career development and early résumé building outside the business.*

- Inside the business, require performance measured against objective standards, reviewed where possible by a qualified non-family superior.

- *Discuss estate planning and management transition issues regularly; and in specific terms.*

THE HEIR(S)-IN-LAW: YOU *THINK* YOU WILL!

There was a time when spouses were chosen for children by their elders— by parents, clergy, or sovereigns. We (most of us, anyway) wouldn't want to return to those days (although there *are* times…).

To put the situation baldly, heirs-in-law in closely held and family businesses (defined, here, as non-owners married to *potential* owners) are perceived as relatively less loyal, less trustworthy, less cooperative, and less committed than their spouses. They come from different families, from different (and sometimes "unusual") cultures. They have different backgrounds and values.

They're, well, just *different.*

The Male Heir-in-Law (The "Vice President")

Sons-in-law of business owners have two unique strikes against them almost from the moment they marry into a family owning a business.

First, they are *potential* gold diggers. This label is only potential, but, unless the son-in-law has a fortune and/or family business of his own, there is always the possibility that someone in the family will or does think, *"That's why he married her."*

This may be seen as an overly harsh view, but it is more the rule than the exception. I hear it often in the form of *"I haven't passed any stock to her because I'm not so sure she won't get a divorce."* The concept raises an image of thousands of Thanksgiving dinners all over America, where family members are looking at the in-law and asking: *"Well, you divorced her yet?"*

The second strike is chalked up in the event the son-in-law joins the business. He wasn't, you see, his wife's best possible choice. She could've done much better, her parents (primarily her father) think, and since he never quite measures up in the family's eyes, he never quite measures up in the business, either.

He begins as a Vice President of [*fill-in the blank*], mostly because his in-laws want to make sure their daughter and grandchildren are provided for adequately. He retires as Vice President (vs. "President" or "Chairman"), because his in-laws with rare exception would find it inconceivable (pun intended) to give the top jobs to in-laws rather than to their own offspring.

If the son-in-law is a key manager in the business, ownership seldom passes to him. The general practice regarding whatever equity is designated for his family is to transfer ownership directly his wife.

It's a sort of informal prenuptial agreement, designed to prevent shares from falling into his hands, even if he is one of, or *the* prime builder of, the value of those shares.

"So what's the difference?" his in-laws ask. *"What's hers is his anyway."* Somehow the ring of truth is hollow. He might well ask in return: *"So what's the difference? What's mine is hers anyway."*

A strong case can be made for creating a growth sharing compensation component for non-family key managers in any closely held company (see *Chapter 6*). An even stronger case can be made for doing this for a son-in-law/manager. In fact, the involved son-in-law is one non-family manager who should be considered for a stock option program. That's right, *real* stock.

But more on this later.

The Female Heir-in-Law ("Mata Hari")

The young woman brave enough to marry into a business-owning family most likely and very quickly becomes a stranger in a strange land. The odds are she doesn't have a family business in her background, and therefore goes through a myth-to-reality transition in the early years of her marriage. The questions she has for her husband are common, and they repeat:

- Why do you have to work every weekend?

- If your Father (Uncle, Brother, etc.) gets on your nerves so much, why don't you just quit?

- Can't we ever go over to your folks' and talk about something besides the business?

- How do you know you'll have ownership if something happens to your Dad (Mom, Uncle, etc.)?

- Everything you build goes to him (or them). When are we going to start building something for ourselves?

And, when she finally gets herself into *extremis*:

- When are you ever going to stand up to that Old Goat?

Business owners might be uneasy around their partners' spouses, but they are *definitely* uncomfortable with their daughters-in-law. Frequently, these misunderstood women develop reputations as "aggressive," "difficult," "greedy," "troublemaking" — hence my nickname for her: "Mata Hari." To listen to the in-laws, one would almost think that sons of business owners are attracted naturally to contrary females.

The reality is something else, entirely. The owner's daughter-in-law is usually just trying to live her life the best way she can, given the tools and knowledge she's been allowed — which are few and none, respectively. Because her husband is waiting for that "some-day," when it will all be his, she sees him spending the best years of his career becoming less defined, more frustrated, and increasingly unemployable outside the business, with no balancing benefit in *actual* equity.

She sees, quite clearly, that the only existing reward system is based more on socialism than sound compensation principles. Her husband is paid according to one or another loopy policy, either equally to all his siblings and/or cousins (to keep a peace that she knows never existed in the first place), or according to the owner's gut feel, a standard that has no correlation to the real world (a guarantee of her increasing feelings of financial insecurity).

She asks, not unreasonably but unrealistically, her husband to explore these issues with his parents and the other owners. He never gets around to it. After a few years, in exasperation, she starts asking the questions herself. That's seen as impertinent, none of her affair, aggressive, even greedy. (And these are only the polite terms.) Her husband, wanting to maintain peace with *all* the people he loves, says little, inadvertently abandoning her to fight the family alone. At least that's how she comes to see it.

If a business weren't involved, the daughter-in-law's plight might simply be seen as a typical example of spouses failing to communicate. Add a business to the equation, however, and suddenly her attitude becomes a key strategic variable.

It's quite simple to understand, really. Mata Hari is the second most powerful person in the family/business system, ranking only below the owners in influence. If she believes she is being treated unjustly, or if she is unhappy about the situation her husband is in, she has very persuasive influence behind closed doors, influence that far outstrips that of her husband's parents.

Machiavelli gave us "The Prince" as a symbol of Byzantine intrigue and scheming. The family business has given us "The Daughter-in-Law." The world inhabited by this woman can be a frustrating, confusing, often frightening one — and it's not made any easier by the appearance to outsiders that she has everything. Her in-laws, of course, tend to assume that she has a lot more than she had before (or could have had anywhere else).

Her husband is the scion of a local economic power. Their financial prospects seem "endless" (not to mention "unearned") to others watching from the outside. Their old friends become more distant as time goes by, usually because they have an overblown picture of how quickly the successor's earnings increase. The successor's wife grows more and more alienated. She's been pigeon-holed on the basis of something over which she has no control.

On top of all this, she and her husband live in entirely different worlds.

His is the heady environment (although far from the "head") of the busines: the worries, the challenges, the emergencies, the successes. His is an absorbing world, which is also exhausting. When he comes home, he wants peace.

She's tired at the end of her day, too, she may even be exhausted from fighting her own career battles, but she still worries and wonders about the unknowns in this business that seems to enfold their lives. What she wants to talk about is "The Company," that institution which represents her financial security, and which absorbs so much of her husband's time, energy, and attention. She wants to talk about it; she wants to know; she wants to share.

But he's tired. The last thing he wants is to relive the conflicts of the day — even those that ended well. She can't know if he doesn't tell her, and usually he doesn't. She's left only with her extremely active imagination.

This woman is a key member of the succession team, but she's often treated with less understanding and consideration than a new employee in the shop. She's taken for granted until she becomes a "Problem."

She's expected to understand, you see. She's expected to follow a whole list of "shoulds:"

- She should stand silently by her spouse as he fights the daily battles for their joint security.

- She should understand when her husband's work days get longer and their time together gets shorter.

- She should understand why, when he's with her, he's not really there.

- She should bite her tongue when something about the business upsets her (it's not her place to complain, it's his).

- She should share the family's love for and commitment to the business, even though she really doesn't understand it and feels excluded.

- She should support him in problems of which she's unaware, cheer victories she doesn't understand, but she shouldn't burden him too much with *her* concerns (they distract him and get him upset).

- She should enjoy and entertain her in-laws, as they do

her, but this should never, *ever,* become clouded by problems which might be occurring in the business.

She should, in short, be all things to all people, but she shouldn't expect anyone to pay attention to her worries or her needs.

What makes this situation so difficult is that usually nobody acknowledges this litany of "shoulds." Or, if they do, they're considered reasonable expectations rather than difficult demands. They're an assumed way of life. So if she balks, she's seen as uncooperative, selfish, obstructive, and even greedy. She's no longer spoken of by name, and in extreme cases is simply referred to as "that woman he married." When that happens, she's lost her struggle to become part of the wider family into which she married.

Her in-laws, at least, feel they have control. If her attitude hurts them or makes them uncomfortable, they at first try to do something about it. They might get angry or they might try harder to make her understand (read: *persuade her to their point of view*). But when this seems to increase the conflict and the misunderstanding, they decide the best course is to ignore her, to let it lie. After all, she doesn't have much real effect on their lives, as long as they can continue to see the grandchildren. Sometimes they're right. Ignoring her avoids causing overt problems. For a time.

She can't ignore *them*, however, and won't. Her husband can't ignore her, even if he sometimes wants to. If the daughter-in-law has problems, she's not going to keep them to herself forever. If she's ignored, the business is going to have problems.

Business owners ignore or mistreat her (albeit unintentionally and unconsciously) at their great peril.

Key Realities for the Successors' Spouses

- Not being "blood" places the heir-in-law always on the periphery of the business-owning family.

- Heirs-in-law in closely held businesses are generally

kept outside the information flow and decision making of the business, despite the fact that in most cases it represents their most significant financial asset.

Implications

- *Think of heirs' spouses as members of the family and take steps to treat them as such, visibly, openly and genuinely.*

- *Take steps to ensure that heirs' spouses have sufficient information to understand the nature and potential of the business asset, and that they have reasonable input to decisions that affect them and their families.*

THE HELP*(LESS)*: *WHO'S* RUNNING *WHAT* SHOW?

Picture yourself as a flight attendant on a DC-10. The plane is well-equipped. You like your job. You want to build your career. You willingly and quite naturally place your life in the hands of the crew in the cockpit. You rarely think about the dangers.

Then, one day, you hear shouts in the cockpit. You wonder about that, briefly, but eventually assume it's nothing and get on with your work. Time passes. Another flight. More shouts. The anxiety increases. Later, on the ground between flights, you see the Captain scowl at his copilot as he stalks off the plane. Still later, once again in the air, there's even more shouting, what sounds like a fist fight. The plane lurches. It dives 10,000 feet, then levels and begins a slow climb, regaining altitude.

And it's *your* job to start the dinner service...

A ridiculous situation? For a flight attendant, maybe, but not so far off for many key employees in closely held businesses.

How Insecurity Can Demotivate

Key employees in family companies, with no blood ties as parachutes, often get airsick in the wind shear of The Boss's whim. Others live in fear of being shot out of the sky by the arrival of "The Kids." The typical result? A desperate search for safety equipment — usually some form of written contract — as a guarantee of continued employment.

A contract might ease the "flight anxiety" somewhat, but it sure won't provide job security. Not the kind the non-family employee wants.

I worked with a closely held distributor a few years ago who recruited one of his outside directors, a close and trusted friend, to work as his CEO. With Jake's blessing, the other directors asked this friend to step in because they could see Jake was burned out. Major personal problems, combined with some numbing business reversals had left him with a short fuse and low self-confidence.

Steve, the new CEO cornered me one morning about three months after taking on the job. He had a problem.

"Jake wants me to turn this place around, and I'm willing to do what it takes, but he's making it almost impossible. I can't get any real direction from Jake because I don't think he knows where he wants this business to go. Even if I had the goals, I'd have to run every decision by him first, which would be okay if *he* then made a decision. He doesn't. He mulls things over for days, tying my hands.

"And Jake's so volatile. I've been trying to get him to sign an employment contract my lawyer drafted for me, but he's resisting. I'll tell you, if I don't get this in writing, I'm afraid he'll fire me the next time he gets mad or depressed. I've seen him do it to others. If it happens, I probably won't even know why.

"Remember, he's got a son and a daughter out there somewhere 'finding themselves.' I wouldn't be surprised if one of them comes back to the shop, and suddenly I'm in training on how to handle expendability."

Steve wasn't in the grip of paranoid delusion. Jake was difficult. He hesitated to make some of the major changes Steve wanted, mostly because they affected old guard employees who'd been with Jake for decades. Also, like most parents, Jake had the potential to become overly generous, should his roving children return, and might treat them better than loyal employees who'd been there, sticking it out year after year.

Still, Jake was a levelheaded and honorable guy. He wasn't consumed by pulling the strings of power. And he had some legitimate concerns, too. Was Steve the right guy? Could Jake trust him with significant capital and the futures of his old, loyal employees?

I asked Steve to show me a copy of the contract he wanted Jake to sign. It was 20 pages long and included provisions for everything but paid emergency foot surgery for his pet Airedale. The contract contained obligations to provide holidays and vacation time, country club dues, automobile reimbursements, first-class air travel, term life insurance, 12 months guaranteed salary in the event of dismissal — with the stipulation that Steve could only be dismissed by a majority *secret* ballot of the Board of Directors!

This really raised my red flags. I was sure they'd *ignited* Jake's. Business owners learn early and often to guard their options, husband their power, and, above all, keep control. (These are, after all, some of the fundamental attractions of business ownership, the freedoms that make all that risk worthwhile.) They hack their businesses out of a precarious jungle, and the prospect of having their hands tied behind their backs — as Steve's Christmas tree contract tried to do — makes them absolutely claustrophobic.

"You're chasing the wrong rainbow," I said to Steve. "Jake's not interested in solving your security problems. He wants you to solve *his* problems."

"That's what I'm trying to do," he replied, "But without a contract, Jake can pull the rug out from under me at any minute. I can't work like that."

"With a contract, he can do the same thing," I said.

Business owners can be as capricious and unpredictable as anyone with significant power, and the non-family key manager can become a victim of the arbitrary use of that power. Still, despite all the downsizing and layoffs, truly effective people are hard to find. Most business owners respond to value-added, and even the most volatile owner will think twice before chopping off the head of one of his best soldiers, which is what I told Steve.

True Security: Delivery and Reward of Performance

"Give this job three more months," I suggested to Steve. "Work with the Board to define performance standards, then ask for the authority you need to meet those standards.

"Meanwhile, have your lawyer pull all the parsley and carrot curls out of the contract draft. Forget the vacations, the club dues, and all the perks. They only confuse the issue and make you sound like a bureaucrat. Instead, set down the performance targets you agree to meet, and define a generous base salary, with an open-ended incentive bonus tied directly to the value you're building for Jake, and some form of non-equity growth participation, like phantom stock.

"Let the salary and bonus be generous enough to cover all those goodies like club dues. Make your golf clubs your business, not Jake's.

"Accept the fact that you're an employee in a family business. That means it's more than a business to you. It's a business with owners whose personal lives can be as much a concern to you as their business decisions. That's a price you've chosen to pay to have the freedom and wider responsibility that comes with close ownership.

"You want security? Do your job better than anyone expected. Ask for severance pay only if you're fired in spite of meeting performance standards. That will seem fair to everybody.

"Show them results, and you'll have no problem selling Jake or the Board on a very generous compensation agreement."

Steve was skeptical. Although it sounded good in theory, he doubted Jake or the Board would go along. Still, he wasn't making any headway doing it his way, so he figured three months wasn't so much to risk. He asked for a special board meeting and laid out his requirements.

"Give me three months," he said, "some targets, and the freedom to move, and if it works, we can talk about a contract."

The other directors caucused with Jake and persuaded him to give it a shot.

For three months, Steve stopped worrying about getting fired and concentrated all his energy on the main and most visible problems: poor sales performance and inadequate customer service.

Once he stopped worrying about his so-called "job security," he was able to act decisively, ignoring worries about what Jake's reaction might be — and, believe me, they had some battles. Steve couldn't solve every problem in three months, but he turned some key things around, visibly and dramatically.

At the next quarterly board meeting, over the objections of his attorney, he presented, along with the improved financials, an employment contract draft that was three pages long. No perks, sidecars, or gingerbread. It locked the company only into:

- Paying him very well for achieving objectives defined by the board

- Hefty severance pay if he was fired while meeting defined performance standards

- A "phantom stock" arrangement, which allowed him to participate in company growth both as a long-term incentive (golden handcuffs), and as an expanding cushion (golden parachute) against Jake's arbitrariness or those Sidewinder missiles from Jake's kids that worried him so much.

Jake and the Board looked over the financial statements, examined the contract, and told Steve he had a deal. They didn't even ask for a non-compete clause. Jake would've preferred not to have a contract (all business owners want to remain as "flexible" as possible), but he really couldn't raise any reasonable objections to what Steve wanted.

Steve has done very well. Even though Jake's son did, in fact, return to the company, and controlling ownership will eventually go to him, Steve's "phantom stock" is appreciating very nicely and he's not complaining. Besides, he recently had two significant job offers, based on his fine performance for Jake. His income and expanding "equity" (he's almost fully vested), as well as the flexibility he has in running the operation, keep him around, but he likes knowing he has other options.

Jake and Steve will always be a little wary of each other, but now they both know they're better off together than apart.

Steve learned a fact of life: employment contracts are a lot like marriage contracts. They may help hold things together by "complicating" a separation, but the real glue comes from keeping oneself "desirable" as a partner, day after day, week after week.

Guaranteed job security exists only in monasteries.

Jake, on the other hand, learned a valuable lesson, too. Effective non-owner key employees can be invaluable to the business, but they tend to be an insecure bunch, tethered to the business with ties a lot flimsier than the blood and sweat holding the owners. I think this was put best by a non-owner, long-term president of a family company I know. As he was approaching his retirement he once said to me that he knew very well that the owner/chairman would never retire, but that he, himself, didn't have that option. *"I'm not family,"* he said, *"and I've known all along what that means."*

Jake realized that Steve wasn't particularly paranoid. He was just feeling defenseless in a risky situation, where he was being asked to stick his neck way out to be a hero. If Jake wanted Steve to solve his problems, he had to help Steve solve some of his own.

Key Realities for the Non-Owner Manager

- A non-owning manager is not an owner, and usually has no

potential for becoming an owner. This situation sets up an automatic disconnect between owners' objectives and key employee objectives.

- A non-owning manager finds that business responsibilities are inevitably intertwined with responsibilities to the owners and their families. The two levels of responsibility frequently conflict, and there is usually no process for resolving the confusion.

Implications

- *Institutionalize trust.* Key employees need information to do their jobs, and suffocate under the veil of secrecy enveloping many closely held companies.

- *Define performance standards.* This is more complicated than setting sales targets. It requires that the owners define their vision for the investment, and that the Board (however it's structured), translates that vision into cash flow and profit targets for management.

- *Compensate performance, not presence.* For the sake of the owners and the key managers, the standards for compensation should be clear, and tied closely to measurable owner-value objectives.

- *Provide an opportunity for sharing in equity growth.* While the most difficult for business owners to accept, this concept is steadily becoming the *sine qua non* for building a sound management team (see *Chapter 6*).

3: The Causes of — and Cures for — Anarchy

> The petroleum marketer needed someone, as he put it, "to help straighten out my kid."
>
> "What's wrong with your son?" was the natural question.
>
> "Nothing. Everything. He wants to add eight more service trucks to the fleet. That's almost a quarter of a million bucks, and he'll do that over my dead body, let me tell you!"
>
> They argued about it all the time, he said. Neither father nor son would budge from his blistered howitzers. The bad blood between them was heating up fast, with the business sinking into paralysis. The Boss saw it as "this asinine disagreement over some stupid trucks, proposed by a cocky kid with no experience in the real world."
>
> His son saw it as a dead hand on the controls: "Dad was great, in his time. Heck, he's *still* smarter than 99% of the people out there.
>
> "But how can I convince him that the *world* has changed? We're fighting battles on battlefields that didn't even exist 10 years ago."

This "case of the $250,000 trucks" has a script that sounds very familiar to anyone who has experience with the management of closely held companies. Irresolvable disagreements and conflicts over tactical decisions tend to dot the owner-management landscape. Over time, they can dominate and paralyze decision making, as this particular dispute did, very predictably.

At this owner's request, I met with him and his son a few weeks later at their offices. We hadn't been seated more than 30 seconds when Dad turned to me, pointed to his son, and said: *"All right, Jonovic. Tell him!"*

I ignored his unique view of consulting. Instead of proceeding with "straightening out the kid," as he expected, I asked the two men to write on slips of paper how much of a financial bet their company could make on a new venture, see that venture fail, and still be around as a viable business. What, I was asking, was their financial "robustness"?

They each wrote out a number, folded their papers at my request, and handed them to me. I shuffled them to add a sense of suspense, then opened the first one. On it, in two-inch lettering, was written "ZERO!!!" (You don't have to guess who that was from.) I opened the second slip.

You guessed it. It read "$250,000."

I wasn't looking for a "right" answer to my question. The exercise wasn't meant to test their knowledge of balance-sheet ratios. It was intended, instead, to demonstrate a key point about their ongoing service truck argument.

The point? They weren't arguing about trucks! Their disagreement was, in fact, about something much more fundamental than equipment.

You guessed right again. They were disagreeing about *risk*, about the long-range objectives and potential of the business. Because they didn't understand the real source of their dispute, they were trapped in an expanding spiral of miscommunication and frustration.

They didn't need strategic planning, at least not at that point. In situations such as this, many business owners and their key people look to strategic planning as a specific cure for "vision" disputes. But that's not the answer, because strategy can't be set in any sensible way without first establishing some form of ownership agreement, an "owner vision," that defines what the owners want *from* — and are willing to give *to* — the investment.

This oil jobber and his son had two separate visions, not a shared one, and this schizophrenia was paralyzing both. They were far from unique in this problem. The lack of a *shared investment strategy* destroys more companies than taxes, competition, recessions and the, uh, ultra-liberal politicians combined.

WHY THINGS GET CONFUSED

In addition to these individual and separate realities, the central players in the closely held business drama also have differing goals and objectives. Sometimes those differences diverge very widely, indeed.

For example, consider a business owned by four major shareholders. Two of the shareholders are owner-managers. They have senior management roles in the business. The other two are not involved at all.

The two owner-managers are working hard to make the business grow. They try to keep their non-involved partners informed, but, you know how it is. The pressure's intense. There's no time. And when they do take the time, Pandora's box tends to open, resulting in involved, seemingly endless discussions about who's paid too much, or why it takes the receptionist so long to answer the phone, or why is depreciation so high, which eat even more time.

The tendency toward fruitless debate is a central problem in most family companies. Whether we're dealing with owners, directors, or key managers, for every person involved, there's usually a different perspective and, hence, a different "plan." Worse, those plans are unwritten, un-discussed, and probably incompatible.

Think about the different roles we play for a minute (see *Figure 3-1)*. First of all, everybody in the owner group can see himself or herself *as an investor* (or a *potential* investor, which includes the

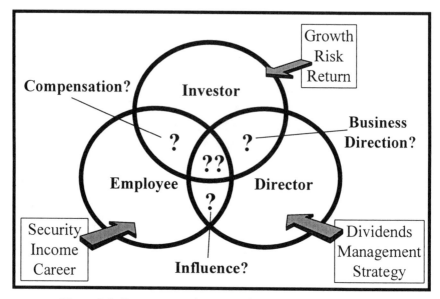

Figure 3-1: Representing the private business "theory of relativity," this diagram shows how the overlapping of key roles owners play in a business can lead to conflict and discord. This overlap happens regularly in businesses where discussions are not separated and focused on questions appropriate to only one of the key roles.

spouses of owners and potential owners). Investors are interested in sufficient cash flow, growth, return, liquidity, all those wealth issues. They also want adequate increase in the value of their investment, preferably at appropriate levels of risk.

Common sense? Natural? Of course. The problem, however, comes when we try to define the exact meaning of adjectives like "sufficient," "adequate," and "appropriate."

The oil jobber who wanted me to straighten out his son was 72 years old. He'd founded the business and functioned as president from its beginning. For most of the 40-plus years since he bought his first delivery truck, he'd filled, by himself, every one of the roles pictured above. Filled them well, too. Just ask him.

As my exercise with the slips of paper showed, however, his

focus as a shareholder had progressively shifted toward the return on his investment, and away from the concept of growth. Nothing wrong with this. After all, a "long-term" investment of $250,000 means something entirely different to a 72-year-old than it does to a 40-year-old (his "cocky kid's" age at the time).

Dad was still majority owner, so of course he played a significant role on the "board" as well. Since he was semi-retired, the career and cash flow (income) issues so important to an employee had become a lot less important to him than they were in his 50s. As a "board" member, his management attitudes concerning future directions of the business, how shareholders should be paid, even who should be running the show, were all valid, given his point in life and past experience. If they lost the business, it was too late for him to start over.

Let's look for a moment at his son. He had a few shares and, therefore, was an owner, too. But his "investor" focus was on growth. Return, given the fact that he was relatively young and a very active employee, tended to take the form of salary, bonus, various perks, and a healthy, growing business. Consequently, when he looked at return, he was doing so more as an employee. Risk was an important issue with him, too, but seemed greater, long-term, if they did *nothing* rather than if they did the *wrong thing*. What if the business were to fail because they were too aggressive? Well, he could always start over.

These meetings — and where they had their conflict — usually took place in the "boardroom." In their case, that happened to be Dad's office, where a "board meeting" was defined by a routine conversation suddenly getting heated and out of hand. They each brought their *valid* perspectives to the conversation, but they failed to recognize not only how different those perspectives were, but, perhaps more importantly, the reason behind and source of those differences. Because of this, their individual goals as investors and as employees overwhelmed any discussion they might have had about "strategy."

This is only one example, but it's all too typical. Should we wonder, then, why most closely held companies don't have real boards or board meetings?

SEPARATING PERSPECTIVES IN BUSINESS DISCUSSIONS

The first step, since any decision-making process requires effective communication, is to eliminate confused perspectives, the principal cause of decision paralysis in the closely held company (*Figure 3-2*).

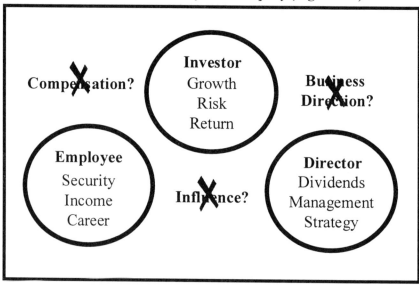

Figure 3-2: Separation of the key roles in formal discussion allows each person to freely express his or her opinion and makes it much more likely decisions will be made, and made objectively, rather than blocked by emotion. Where this discipline exists in a company, recurring disputes about compensation, relative influence, and business direction tend to disappear.

Separation of perspectives is essential. Consider what happens when discussions of business issues allow the players to take any point of view they want. Where *investors confuse themselves with directors*, we find disagreements about business direction issues. The greater this overlap, the more paralyzed decision-making becomes.

Where *investors confuse themselves with employees,* we run

into all sorts of "avid discussions" (to use the polite term for what really happens). For example, a favorite "discussion" topic is compensation. The concepts of dividend and salary get hopelessly confused, "fair" and "equal" replace common sense and money becomes the root of all evil.

Where *employees confuse themselves with directors,* we have blurred lines of authority and power conflicts: *"Sure, I'm just the purchasing manager, but I damn well have some say in who's going to be my boss,"* or *"I don't care if he is my boss, it's my company, too, and I'm going to do what I darn well please."*

Finally, where all these perspectives overlap simultaneously in one meeting or discussion, we have a preview of World War III.

What should we do? True agreement emerges out of a careful separation of these roles (see *Figure 3-3*). It emerges out of formal

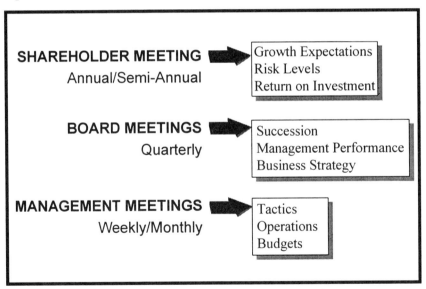

Figure 3-3: Not all bureaucracy is dysfunctional. Some is essential to the smooth functioning of an organization. Founding entrepreneurs can afford to discuss issues with themselves, on the fly, while shaving. Multi-owner businesses have to be a lot more formal than that, regularly holding the meetings shown above (at least).

meetings and discussions, with each level setting directions and objectives for the level below. The same people can, and frequently (but not always) do it all. They just have to change hats. This requires, unfortunately, a little bureaucracy — primarily the establishment of a formal schedule of meetings, each concentrating on a different strategic level:

The Investor Meeting

Investors set standards of investment return, growth, and liquidity — the broadest strategic level (what are the purposes for fighting this war?). Their discussion of these important issues must be prior to all other long-range decisions made in the business.

The Board Meeting

Directors translate those standards into business policies and strategies, and then ensure selection of a management team to make it happen — general operating strategy (where do we concentrate our forces, who will lead them, what are their broad objectives?).

Board meetings proceed on much the same basis as advisory board meetings (see *Appendix A-8*), but they are naturally more formal and more strategic in outlook. Much of the input expected from a board arises from the board's function, and these functions can be found in the example board policy in *Appendix A-10*.

The Management Meeting

Managers/employees go out on the front line and implement tactics to achieve the strategic goals they're given — day-to-day operating procedures (how can we accomplish the broad objectives set by the board, and who will carry them out?).

The central purpose for this bureaucratization is to separate the "hats" under which people think, discuss, and operate. Using the specific meeting format appropriate for the level of discussion at hand, we vastly increase the chances that we will objectively come to intelligent, effective decisions.

Obviously, simply holding more meetings isn't going to be the panacea for all business problems. Formalization merely provides a framework within which the right questions can be asked, effective discussion is possible, and sound decisions can be made.

To make sure these meetings work, to make sure, in fact, that they are even held, one more important piece of infrastructure is necessary: the right *help*.

TODAY

.

4: The Right Advice

"How could you have possibly spent $35,000 on a shareholder meeting?"

Sally flinched. Her father's outburst was totally unexpected. Worse, she didn't even know what he was talking about.

"I don't understand," she said.

"Here, look at this," he said, tossing a sheaf of papers across his desk. Sally could see immediately that it was an invoice from the accounting firm. When she picked it up, the bottom figure jumped out like an accusing finger. $22,000! She couldn't believe what she was reading.

"And that's only from the accountants," her father growled. "The law firm adds another $13,000 to that!"

Sally's shock was slowly giving way to understanding and with that came acute embarrassment. She'd been given the responsibility for putting together the first real shareholder meeting they'd ever had, and decided to make it a real meeting with real substance. She brought in the advisors and told them she wanted overview presentations of the existing estate plan and a discussion of business value.

"I'm glad you're finally doing this," the accountant had agreed right away. "There's too much confusion among the shareholders, and this is stuff they need to know."

"Absolutely," the attorney said.

So, they went ahead, putting together their presentations. The shareholder meeting was right on target, got right to the important issues; the shareholders, Sally's siblings and cousins, congratulated her afterward on an excellent meeting.

That was three weeks ago. Now this! More than $30,000 to

present an existing set of facts...

"...and from now on," her father was saying, "I want to approve any work you do with any of the advisors, you understand?"

Sally looked up at him, her eyes glistening.

"Oh, I understand perfectly," she replied, embarrassment now turning to anger. "Don't you worry. They'll never give us a problem again."

Sally learned a lesson, all right. Open yourself to the outside world, and you're going to get burned, badly burned. Unfortunately, she's going to be a good student.

As I noted in *Chapter 1*, closely held companies are misnamed. More appropriately, although regrettably, they could be called "hermetically sealed" companies.

At some critical point in the history of every successful, private company, the level of knowledge and skill inside the business is overtaken and overwhelmed by the rising tide of demands and challenges imposed by the outside environment. Unfortunately, just when outside understanding and knowledge is needed the most, it is usually the most inaccessible or, worse, inadequate — as it is about to become in the case of Sally's company because it is perceived as "too expensive."

The closely held company's need for outside review is well-accepted and widely known, but filling that need has not been an easy task. As I noted earlier, I've been among those who've urged the creation of a formal, outside board of directors as a potential solution. However, today I don't consider the board to be the best place to begin bringing outside advice and review to a closely held company, and business owners tend to agree.

The reaction of one of my clients to the suggestion of forming an outside board is a good example. His words were simple and direct:

"No [*expletive*] way!"

We were working on a number of leadership transition issues with him and his two partner brothers. It was going along smoothly until the possibility of instituting a real board was considered. The chairman dug in his heels, firmly opposed to the formation of a real board.

I wasn't surprised. In fact, I agreed with him. Although he and his brothers had a large distributorship employing more than 200, neither they nor the business was ready for outside directors. What we created instead was an advisory board, which operated successfully for two years, solving technical problems involving stock transfer and retirement funding, before evolving into a real board.

My years of consulting and board experience have made it evident to me that most family businesses require significant evolution before they can benefit from an outside board. (See *Appendix A-9* for a discussion of reasons why outside boards fail.) A board does not become relevant or potentially effective, really, until the company is well through the "threshold" transition between entrepreneurial venture and professional management. During this transitional phase (what I refer to as the "threshold" period — when business is thriving but still heavily dependent upon the strong leadership of entrepreneurial owners), an advisory board, or advisory council, is much more useful for responding to both business and family needs.

WHAT HELP DO WE REALLY NEED?

This concept of *threshold* transition requires a closer look (see *Figure 4-1*). Family and closely held businesses usually go through a difficult period as they grow beyond the founder's direct influence, but have not yet fully professionalized management. This is the "threshold" period. Some companies take longer — perhaps even generations — to cross the threshold than others. Size seems to have relatively little to do with how quickly the transition can or must occur. Even very large organizations, for example, can go on functioning for quite some time with relatively weak middle management.

Prior to reaching the threshold, most entrepreneurial ventures are primarily self-sufficient. For the most part, the typical entrepreneur (and his successor managers, if they retain the founder's style)

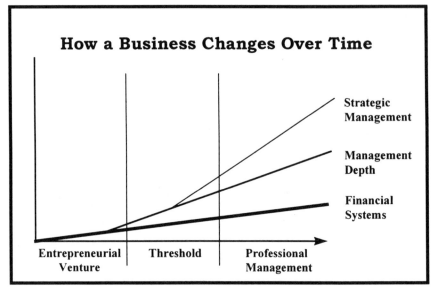

How a Business Changes Over Time

Strategic Management

Management Depth

Financial Systems

Entrepreneurial Venture | Threshold | Professional Management

Figure 4-1: Businesses go through three developmental periods as they become successful. It's only later, on the road to professional management that the concept "strategy" even begins to take on importance.

relies on drive, adrenaline, and persistence to survive, punch through barriers and reach goals. True outside review, by contrast, would be analytical, critical, questioning — in obvious and direct conflict with the entrepreneur's style. Therefore, the hermetic seal (*I do it alone, I do it my way, and nobody but me needs to know about it*) is usually very functional in the early years.

In a perfect world, criticism and healthy questioning can be intellectually stimulating, not to mention helpful. In the real world of the entrepreneurial venture, however, survival is a white-knuckle thing, like barnstorming. To the entrepreneur's way of thinking, the fine points of flying can be studied later. He has no need for back seat instructors right now. Just give him a good mechanic or two.

As *Figure 4-1* illustrates, there's little in the way of financial systems, no management depth to speak of, and "strategic" boils down to "next Saturday." Growing value in the new business is the job of the entrepreneur, probably best accomplished in his solitary determination, focused on his dream and fueled by his sweat. Outsiders could tend to distract him, drain precious time and energy and even clutter up his decision making.

In the *threshold* stage, the business owner's afterburners typically begin to sputter just when he needs extra thrust to handle the dangerous turbulence being thrown at him by accelerating growth. It's at this point, he usually starts looking for technical solutions to technical problems, as well as the people to fly shotgun for him and sweep for strategic land mines like significant competitor moves or changes in commodity markets.

"Loneliness at the top" during this threshold period between entrepreneurial venture and a professionalized company takes on an entirely new dimension for the now-successful entrepreneur. Not only does the buck still stop in his lap, but now flak is whizzing by on all sides and the dials on the control panel are starting to spin. Lacking a well-developed management team, the harried entrepreneur has nobody to watch his back or help fly the plane — help he now seriously needs.

As successful growth continues — growth which almost always requires an evolving management team — The Boss and his managers find themselves increasingly looking farther ahead of the aircraft. Quick responses are becoming more and more difficult to achieve as the asset base grows and problems become more complex. Now, both The Boss and the management team develop an increasing need for some sort of "ground control," somebody to help with the bigger picture, with strategy. Clearly, the operation has changed fundamentally, and because of that change, the need for help also has changed significantly (see *Figure 4-2*).

In the beginning, the new entrepreneur mostly needs room to run. "Leave me alone!" is the battle cry. As success and growth begin to occur, however, the need for professionals like accountants, attorneys, estate planners, and industry consultants, also begins to grow.

Near the end of the early phase, another form of help — that

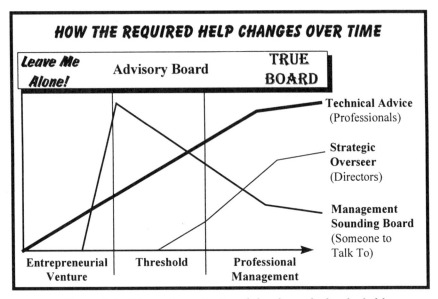

HOW THE REQUIRED HELP CHANGES OVER TIME

Figure 4-2: Since the majority of family and closely held companies are either in the entrepreneurial or threshold phases of their development, a formal outside board is not the best source of help. In the early years, with the exception of a few professional advisors, the founders are best left alone. During the threshold period, a group of professional advisors, successful business people, even informed friends and fellow owners can work very well in the context of an advisory board. Only once the business is truly professionalized, is it ready for a real board.

"somebody to talk to" — becomes a need that stays relatively strong through the threshold. Professional advisors aren't enough to help with operating problems of the threshold company like dealing with buying groups or fighting OEM margin squeezes. For growth companies in changing industries, the appropriate sounding boards are generally individuals who have in-depth knowledge of the workings of the markets served by the business and specific characteristics of the owner's industry.

Thus, through the threshold phase, most owner-managers can get more benefit from technical professionals or industry peers than from "outside" directors. (In some industries, for example, groups of CEOs who get to know each other at association meetings but aren't in direct competition serve this function; they form review groups that periodically descend upon one of their members en masse to evaluate his or her business.)

Beyond industry, product, and market issues, other important issues arise during the threshold period that require specific professional expertise of advisors (see *Figure 4-3*, which shows where advisors can have input to the value management process). For example, a company will almost always need help in bringing the shareholders together in agreement on goals and objectives. As we've already seen,

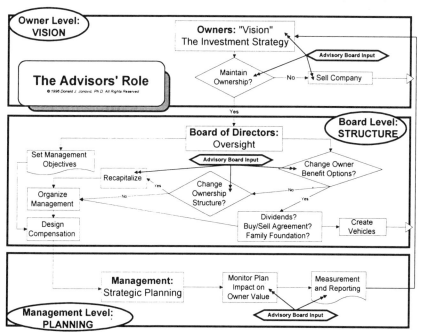

Figure 4-3: This flow diagram, first discussed in the Introduction, shows where advisors are properly involved in the key decision areas impacting the management of owner value. (See Chapter 5 for a discussion of managing shareholder vision, Chapter 6 for approaches to management goals and compensation, and Chapter 7 for a discussion of ownership benefit and transfer planning priorities.) The input of advisors and/or directors (exactly which depends on the stage of evolution of the company), is needed throughout this process, helping the owners and management with issues they may not be qualified to address on their own.

shareholders must separate their overlapping roles as owners, directors, employees, and family members before they can discuss and agree on common strategic goals. Frequently, they need to develop formal agreements defining their expectations of each other and outlining procedures, such as buy/sell agreements, in the event of disruption or disagreement.

Family companies in transition usually need intensive help, too, in planning management succession. Success brings with it the serious requirement to begin separating the concerns of ownership from the concerns of management before they become hopelessly and disastrously confounded with each other. The separation is not natural, but in most cases possible if decision-making is structured the right way. The process requires thinking beyond the present quarter, defining responsibilities, setting up viable measures of performance, instituting a reasonable and understandable compensation system, and establishing a workable management structure.

The help of formal directors is a capstone need. Proper use of competent professional advisors throughout the threshold period can help business owners in transition to become the professional organization that can truly benefit from outside directors.

THE DYSFUNCTIONAL OWNER/ADVISOR RELATIONSHIP

In most closely held companies, however, there are major barriers to using professional advisors effectively. Business owners, in general, consider their professional advisors to be little more than a necessary evil — necessary because (in the business owner's mind) the lawyers and accountants have succeeded in constructing a world too complicated for a normal person to navigate safely.

To the business owner's way of thinking, advisors are an "evil" because:

- They don't understand the real world of the business owner,

- They are reactive rather than proactive, and

- They are far, far too expensive.

Professional advisors — principally accountants, attorneys, and life underwriters — and their business-owner clients often remind me of awkward boys and girls at the high school sock hops of my teens. The clients line one side of the gymnasium, the advisors stand along the wall on the other, and they giggle at each other across the empty dance floor. The future depends on their getting together successfully, yet they never have the nerve to cross the floor and really dance.

Instead, I am often approached by business owners asking if there are any good books on estate planning. With a picture in my mind of all the heavy books in the tax specialist's library, my response is usually something like, *"You might as well tell me you have a tumor on your cerebellum and want a good book on self-administered brain surgery."*

Why don't business owners and their advisors get together and dance? Principally, for the three reasons listed above, but in reverse order of importance. (This is not my personal judgment. I'm simply restating what my clients and other business owners and professional advisors have told me over the years.)

It's essential for all of us to understand these issues in order to resolve and get beyond them because effective advisory relationships are so critical to the future of the family and closely held business. In fact, building successful advisory relationships is certainly a key to managing owner value, long term.

Problems with Fee Structure

They're too d...ned expensive!

First in importance is the issue of cost. Business owners, consciously or unconsciously, tend to see hourly fees and insurance commissions as fundamental conflicts of interest. Why, the business owner asks, should I have to pay someone for how long it takes him to get something done? That's like buying a car by the pound.

The insurance agent and estate planner may try to skate free of the hourly fee complaint by saying they do most of their work at risk. They may try, but it won't save them from the client's displeasure and distrust. *You want to know why I have a problem with you?*, the business owner asks. It's because I have to pay a high premium to cover all that "at risk" work you do for others who don't buy from you in the end. How is that fair? Why is that good business?

Accountants and lawyers, on the other hand, are trapped in their own accounting systems and compensation structures. Many of them agree with the business owners' complaints, but are having a hard time changing a hidebound practice.

But change they must, because clients (read: customers) are beginning to insist on a one-to-one correlation between *value received* and *fees paid* for services. In the coming years, I'm convinced, we will come to think of retainer arrangements, quoted project fees, and flat commission structures as commonplace, and hourly fees will be an arcane curiosity. Until then, however, we need effective, interim solutions, one of which I'll discuss below in the context of advisory boards.

The Advisor's "Reactive" Nature

Accountants are bean counters, historians. Lawyers are always looking for ways to cover their butts. The only original ideas I ever get from them are the ones I bring up in the first place.

These complaints begin to sound like commercial jingles, they're repeated so often. Like jingles, they have some component of truth, but only some.

I've had the good fortune to work closely with many fine attorneys, accountants, and life underwriters over the years. I agree that they tend to be conservative, more reactive than proactive, but often for good reason.

To be a proactive advisor, one first must be in the position to understand the problem — to know what it is you're talking about. In the case of the business-owner client, that means knowing all there is to know about the situation, or at least all that's important to know. Sounds sensible and reasonable, right? But is it simple? Hardly ever. It's not unusual, for example, for an attorney to be asked to design an estate plan, but not be given all the facts (things like the clients' asset holdings, their value, and even insurance in force) he needs to do the job. It's not unusual for an accountant to be asked to review management accounting needs, never having met many of the managers. It's tough under those circumstances to come forward, confidently and aggressively, with a full-blown recommendation.

If advisors and their clients are ever going to dance, let alone get into step with each other, we will have to find a way to educate the advisors on the nature of the client business. An advisory board provides the perfect opportunity for this education.

The Advisor's Business Naïveté

The trouble with accountants (lawyers, etc.) is that they don't understand my business.

There are right and wrong sides on this one, too. It's true that many professional advisors don't have an adequate understanding of many of their clients' businesses, but seldom is this because the advisors simply don't care to learn.

More likely, it's the business owner's reaction to the other complaints — high expense which leads to tepid advice — that's the main cause of this general ignorance. This vicious cycle comes full circle when the client, believing the advice to be lacking in quality and not worth the cost, fails to use (and therefore fails to inform) the advisor.

I've yet to meet a student who could pass a final if he didn't have the texts, and the teacher never let him into the class.

Resolving these issues is crucial. Ignored, as they generally are today, they impose significant negative effects on businesses and the economy. Such a consequence when combined with the general penchant toward secrecy in the closely held business, makes it obvious why "hermetically sealed" is a more apt description than "closely held."

Well, if we are to preserve owner value in our closely held businesses, we must break that hermetic seal. We must seek the input of effective advice and prudent counsel to shareholders, owner-managers, and management teams in closely held businesses. The simplest and most effective way that I've found to do this is to form an *advisory board.*

CREATING AND USING AN ADVISORY BOARD

To repeat an important fact: family and closely held companies in transition face many questions they have neither the experience nor the expertise to answer. These are questions of successor competence, relative rights and benefits of owner-managers, selection of future key managers (including the issues of nepotism), and how to provide for the sensible, secure retirement of the present owner(s).

Further, the process of selecting new leaders, providing for retiring leaders, and all the general issues of family fairness must be managed in a way that is integrated with everything from estate planning to compensation systems to projections of future business value.

Along with a succession plan, agreement also must be reached on ownership transfer. This is not merely a question of estate planning, although the legal and tax elements of the transfer are critical and often complex. There are also questions to be answered concerning the ultimate ownership structure, who will have voting power and control, and what capitalization strategies and buy/sell agreements are appropriate.

An advisory board that is properly constructed with qualified professionals is an excellent vehicle for accomplishing such things. The work needed is exactly the kind of work the advisors do every day of their professional lives. All we need to do is bring them together so we can leverage their experience and knowledge. Here are some specifics:

Who: Advisory Board Membership

During the threshold period, when all of the basic issues mentioned earlier are being dealt with, the business owner will benefit most if he seeks guidance from highly skilled professionals in law, accounting, insurance, and family business management. Such professionals working with the owners — and one another — as an "advisory board" are most qualified to lay the track for

Attorney

The "Core" Advisory Board

CLU/Financial Planner

Accountant

Figure 4-4: The most basic advisory board consists at least of the key professionals, as above, together with the owner-manager(s). They should address the fundamental requirements of owner value management, such as sound shareholder agreements, an investment strategy, and strategic compensation. Once these are met, the structure of the advisory board can become more operational and/or strategic in nature, depending on need, and frequently evolves into a true outside board.

professionalization of a business. Such a "board" may consist of an accountant, an attorney, the senior owner-managers, a family business specialist, perhaps an industry consultant, and, possibly, a representative of non-participating shareholders. The professional advisors usually form the core of such a board.

Further, through the threshold transition, a family business consultant can help resolve family issues and familiarize family members with their roles in the new structure. This involvement can be short-term or long-term, depending on need.

How: Advisory Board Costs

Since perceived excessive cost is the primary reason business owners have difficulty using their advisors effectively, a well-designed advisory board must be structured to eliminate this problem as a concern.

The most efficient way to do this is to establish a retainer arrangement with the key advisors on the team.

Retainers are set in frank conversations, client to advisor, about the need for general help, the essential nature of cost control, and the advisor's legitimate income requirements. An advisory board relationship is not the same as a client relationship. It is a joint commitment to mutual education and general deliberation over general problems for the purpose of making it possible that the issues critical to the ongoing successful operation of the business will be recognized and properly addressed. The retainer is to cover the *board relationship*. Specific *client relationship* issues (e.g., contract drafting, litigation, patent applications) are "off-line" from the board and, therefore, billed separately, preferably through some form of pre-defined project fee or, at least, on a project-by-project basis.

Under the retainer arrangement, the owner should be able to feel free to call the advisor to inform him on or explore general issues. Periodic meetings, say three to five per year, should also be covered, as should preparation for those meetings.

But enough retainer *theory*. Business owners like to get right to the bottom line: just what kind of "retainer" are we talking about? It does, as most realize, depend on the nature of the business, but a good rule of thumb is the retainer should be equivalent to the compensation of the CEO for a similar number of days' input. To put it another way, the number of advisor-days required could be estimated, and multiplied by the equivalent daily salary of the company's top officer. If the number of meetings involved is unpredictable, a proportion of that same number can be used as a per diem for each meeting beyond, say, the primary four or five regular advisory board meetings. This per diem is intended to cover any meeting preparation time that might be required. Since advisory board service is general in nature, preparation time should not generally be extensive.

Let's say, for example, that a CEO of a closely held company is paid a base salary of $260,000 per annum. Assuming 260 working days in a typical year (ignoring the six days a week, 14+ hours daily reality of many entrepreneurial executives), that's about $1,000 per day. An advisory board expecting to meet four times annually would, therefore, involve a retainer of $4,000 per year, per advisor. Committee and other special meetings could carry a per diem of, say, $1,000. Travel expenses would also be covered.

There are other possible approaches to setting retainers, of course. Often, for example, owners will treat the advisory board as an expense item on the income statement, and budget the total cost at 1% or .5% of sales, or whatever is comfortable. This dollar amount is then allocated per advisor as retainer and expense reimbursement. Still, others do something as simple as pull a number out of the air because it seems "about right." Since business owners are very sensitive to the value of money, such "gut" retainers are often appropriate to the situation.

Why would any successful advisor work for a retainer that almost always comes in significantly less than what would be charged if the time were billed on a traditional hourly basis? Because the advisory board relationship allows a much more intimate relationship with the client, a greater chance to be involved in (and bill) technical work beyond the board relationship, and the probability that the extra work will be more cost effective (hence profitable), thanks to greater knowledge of the client and the situation.

Additionally, an advisor serving on a closely held business board is learning a business and an industry, valuable education worth a bit of discounted fee "tuition." And not to be overlooked is the stimulation and satisfaction to be gained from the positive sparks generated by a group of dedicated professionals working at what they know best in a setting designed to get things done. In two words, this spells "job satisfaction."

What: Advisory Board Responsibilities and Objectives

Perhaps the greatest value of an advisory board through the threshold phase of business evolution is the assurance of continuity and coordination. Too often in family business transitions, the experts are allowed only to give advice in separate compartments, usually without a big-picture understanding. What work is done usually moves slowly, by fits and starts, because there is no formal process to manage it.

By setting up an advisory board that meets regularly, with agendas and minutes *(see Appendix A-8 for examples)*, the owners ensure continuity in attention to the issues, coordinated action, and implementation of decisions. The owners also become comfortable with the notion of formal review by outsiders, which paves the way for the long-run ideal of a true outside board as the company becomes increasingly professionalized.

SIGNS THAT YOU'RE READY FOR AN OUTSIDE BOARD

Formal boards of outside directors become appropriate when an organization has achieved, or is coming close to achieving, "professionalization." Getting there requires the passing of a number of essential milestones:

- Adequate, formalized shareholder (e.g., partner or buy/sell) agreements.

- Owners' agreement on goals and objectives for the business as an investment — growth objectives, tolerable risk levels, returns expected, etc.

- The beginnings, at least, of a plan for scheduling and funding the transition of management and ownership from the present to the successor generation.

- Timely, accurate accounting information in a form that facilitates planning, operational decision-making, and performance review (for example, operating and capital budgets, weekly and monthly key results reports).

- Strong, coordinated middle management operating on incentive compensation directed by performance goals.

These are the primary goals that the advisory board should help the business achieve. While every closely held company needs some form of outside review, an advisory board can get the owner-managers ready for the kind of teamwork a real board requires. Advisory boards provide a valuable transition phase for most closely held businesses — getting them to open up, getting them to really use their advisors, getting them to actually do the work and planning that needs doing.

This is the dance. When (and if) the owners are ready for marriage (a real board) they'll know it. Once the advisory board has done its job, the outside board will actually have something to direct.

5: Owner Vision: the "Investment Strategy"

"Any further discussion?" the Chairman asked.

"Well, I feel awful saying this," Dorothy responded, "but we're voting to approve a budget, here, and I don't think anybody on this board, including the Chairman, whose budget it is, believes it."

"Wait just a minute, Dot," her brother, Paul (The Chairman) interrupted. "You implying we're sandbagging the budget?"

Dorothy turned to him, flushed and uncomfortable.

"I'm not sure what 'sandbagging' means, Paul. And I'm not saying you're trying to put something over. Please, I'm just pointing out that, year after year, we miss our budgeted profits by a mile. You always have a justification, and maybe you're right, but why should we take a budget seriously?"

"We use the profits for other things than net income," Jim Greene, the CFO, said. "Acquisitions, capital expenditures, all aggressively expensed to reduce taxes."

"But that doesn't change the fact that we're not making money," Dorothy countered, some anger now replacing embarrassment on her face.

"But we are! You just can't understand accounting," Paul shouted.

"I can understand anemic S-corp payouts," Dorothy's husband shouted back. "You can call it anything you want, Paul, but this company is just not giving us a return on our investment. It's a toy for you and a liability for us."

In the silence following her husband's outburst, Dorothy

looked around the board table. Each of the directors (most of them her siblings) looked worried and confused.

"See," she said, "this is why I feel I can't bring up my concerns. They just cause trouble."

One of the principal reasons why board meetings are seldom held in closely held businesses is the painful way previous meetings ended. It's not raising concerns that causes trouble. What causes trouble is the almost complete inability to deal with concerns like Dorothy's in a constructive way.

It's likely that Paul and his managers have a perfectly clear (to them, at least) business vision. What this ownership group lacks, as most do, is a clear *owner* vision.

Many people, when they hear a business term like "vision" or "vision statement," think of grand proclamations in some academician's business theory course. Does anybody really take them seriously?

Some do. Many don't. Perhaps they don't because vision setting is seen as just so many words on paper — a meaningless wish list that takes valuable time to prepare with no tangible results.

Well, we're not in the pointless exercise business. The "owner vision" I'm referring to here is an investment strategy that is central to business survival — a practical kind of "vision" that addresses the very purpose of our business.

We must come to terms with fundamental issues that divide us as owners. We must find ways to meld our individual perspectives into agreement on goals and direction for the *investment* the business represents. That agreement will make up our investment strategy, which, in essence, is a clear definition of the true purpose of the business. The agreement among all owners on an investment strategy is the most important, fundamental factor in preserving owner *value* in a closely held business. Without it, it is almost impossible to build and sustain a successful business strategy.

"If two people in a business agree on everything," Henry Ford once said, "one of them is superfluous." In other words, disagreement among thoughtful people is inevitable, but that doesn't have to mean anarchy. Disagreement, in fact, should help us come to ever more effective agreements, since, properly managed, two heads are usually better than one.

We've looked at the perspective differences that can cloud the discussions of owners and shareholders, and the need to separate the investor, director, and employee perspectives through a formalized meeting procedure (see *Chapter 3).*

Next, a decision-making process is required. "Process" is a bureaucrat's word. Consultants use it a lot, too. So do academics who use it as a mantra, a liturgy. Business owners, however, hate process.

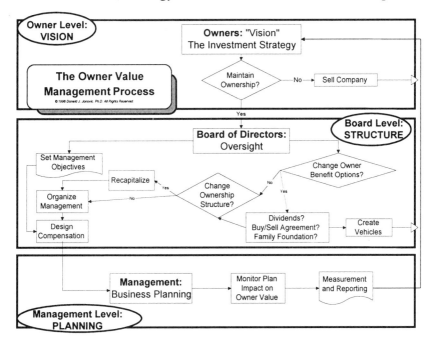

Figure 5-1: *Managing owner value is a way of life which ties together decisions on the owner, board, and management levels. Decision-making on each level must proceed simultaneously with, and in light of, decisions on other levels. This is a growth process, the effectiveness of which will evolve with time and experience.*

Why the difference between theorists and entrepreneurs? They each have a different Pole Star. Theoreticians think long-term. The business owner is firmly fixed on today. Process is not proactive, and it doesn't respond to events. This strikes the business owner as suicidal. If he doesn't see and smother the brush fire when it first flares, it will consume him; the long term will hardly matter.

We each use the tools that work for us. And we should continue to use them. What business owners need as they grow is not a different world view. What they need is *an expanded world view and a larger toolbox.*

To manage success, we must by definition think more in the longer term. It's essential to look ever farther into the future in order to find the right questions to ask. It's also necessary to develop some pigeon holes, a taxonomy, to help us sort out, in a sensible way, the growing number of questions that do and will arise.

Over the years, I've helped business owners face and solve a variety of issues. In almost every case, resolution of issues related to owner value proved to be fundamental to long-term business health, as well as to owner satisfaction and overall owner and family harmony.

In working through these challenges with many businesses and clients, I have seen the evolution of a familiar pattern. It begins with issues that seem, in the eyes of the owners, impossible to resolve. The questions at first appear to be overwhelming, not even approachable, but as we work through them, piece by piece, connections emerge. Logical links usually exist among problems to be addressed. These point to paths to follow in solving them. This process is described by the flow diagram briefly referred to in the *Introduction* and in *Chapter 4*, and reproduced above (*Figure 5-1*).

Don't be put off by the seeming complexity. When broken down into its component parts, the flow chart is simply a summary of actions and decisions taken on the three fundamental levels of any business: the *owner* level (vision), the *board* level (structure), and the *management* level (planning). This chapter will focus on the first of these — owner vision, defined through the investment strategy.

DEVELOPING THE *OWNER VISION*

The most fundamental step, bringing the owners together in their strategy for the investment the business represents (*Figure 5-2*), is usually done at meetings of owners and/or shareholders. Developing this vision is the principal purpose of annual meetings of shareholders, or at least it should be. The questions raised should address such issues as return on investment, value, growth rates, risk tolerance, and corporate values. These must be answered *by the owners* and, although outsiders can offer significant help here, such questions cannot be delegated to others.

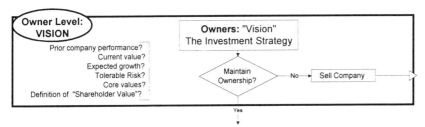

Figure 5-2: *This first portion of the "process" diagram focuses on the critical decisions owners must make about their investment. The role of advisors and other outsiders can be particularly critical here, since one of the fundamental decisions to be made is whether or not to continue ownership of the business.*

Owners and/or shareholders of closely held businesses usually want to increase the value of their investments. There's seldom much disagreement over that issue. Where we run into considerable trouble is in the follow-up questions: what exactly is "value," and what do we consider an acceptable "increase"?

Look again at *Figure 5-2*, at the list of questions to the left of the *Owners: Vision* box. To answer questions about "value" and "increase," these probes are essential. Seldom, however, do shareholders carry on these discussions in any objective way.

- *How has this business performed as an investment?*
  Most of us check our mutual funds and the stock ticker
  on a daily basis. A lot less often, if ever, do we look at
  the *investment performance* of our businesses. Sure, the
  income statement is always an agenda item, but there's
  a vast difference between "net income" and "return on
  investment." In the epigram that opened this chapter,
  for example, Dorothy and her husband are convinced
  their company is not providing an adequate return.
  Based on what evidence? A "low" net income. The
  CFO tried to explain the returns that were coming in
  "above the line," but that offered little consolation to
  Dorothy who was probably looking for distributions in
  the form of dividends, or, at least, some visible increase
  in retained earnings.

- *What is the current value of the business?* Before we
  can even begin to calculate return on investment, we'd
  better agree on what that investment actually is. Accountants have a ready answer: book value. The rest of
  the world has to struggle with reality.

- *What growth rate is desired and possible?* The two
  concepts must be kept closely together. We can desire
  a growth of 25% annually, but turning that growth into
  reality without huge capital infusions to fund acquisitions and/or expansion may be very difficult. Are the
  implications of growth expectations understood by all
  owners? Do we have the will and the wherewithal to
  achieve what we want?

- *What level of risk are we willing to tolerate as investors?* Risk comes in many forms. Business owners face
  liability risks, risks to capital, structural risks, environ-
  mental risks. Many of these can reach right through the
  corporate "veil" into the owner's personal pockets. Few
  owner groups take the time to both fully analyze all the

major risks they face, *and* define common levels of acceptability for each. While much of "risk" is hard to quantify, certain variables covering significant aspects of it can be discussed, defined, and agreed upon by owners. What leverage or debt-to-equity ratio is comfortable for us, for example? What level of insurance coverage can we live with?

- *What are our core values as owners?* This is a "soft" question, but it has some very hard implications. For example, I am a director of a company that continues to invest in a segment of the business that provides less return on its assets than could be realized elsewhere. They have agreed, as partners, that they will continue with this business because of the benefit it brings to children, something that has been a core value of their family since the company was founded more than 60 years ago.

- *How will we define "owner value" in the future?* If our ultimate goal is to preserve and build owner value, it's fairly obvious that we'd better make sure we all have the same definition of what constitutes "value." From this fundamental definition will spring everything starting with our decision to keep or sell the business, through our planning and budgeting process, to the system we use to compensate our management team.

The fundamental decisions at this level, which can only be considered once the key questions have been answered, is *whether or not to maintain the investment, accept the risk, and keep the business.* There is no law of nature that decrees a closely held business must, or even should be preserved. It's a decision related to *owner value,* and how to maximize value given owner needs and objectives.

When the meaning of "owner value" is not defined by an owner group, all sorts of emotional and financial havoc can be wreaked. I've known business owners who hold onto businesses long past their company's peak in market value because they hold out the hope that someone in the family will get interested someday in taking it over. I've also seen expanding businesses with great earning power sold to meet the personal cash needs of a minority of owners.

Otherwise healthy family relationships can be destroyed by trying, year after increasingly stressful year, to preserve a business weighed down by dysfunction and brimming with conflict. (*"It would kill_____ if we failed."*) In a different but equally disastrous scenario, aggressive and talented owner-managers can destroy value for all owners through excessive focus on growth. (*"I know we're not making money now, but we can fix that by leveraging up and buying market share."*)

Defining a jointly accepted meaning for owner value, difficult though that can be, *is the first and most fundamental strategic decision to be made by a closely held company.* Unfortunately, it's usually one of the last decisions to be made, when, far from being "strategic," the main purpose of defining owner value is to determine damages in litigation.

Getting back to Dorothy's problem with her brother, theirs is an example of an attempt at such a definition at a family business board meeting. It failed because she and her brother were confusing the investor and manager perspectives. They *thought* they were having a board meeting. Instead, they were in the middle of a combined shareholder-management meeting. Had their meeting been defined, instead, as an *owner* or *shareholder* meeting, with the appropriate agenda set beforehand, the discussion (with the essential help of the advisors) could have been much more productive.

ESTABLISHING THE DEFINITION OF VALUE

Anybody familiar with formal business valuations knows that the process is composed of equal parts of science and art. This is not the place to get into arcane methodologies for placing values on companies, but it is important to think about specific assumptions we may be (or should be) making about what the key components of value are in our specific business.

At the two extremes of the valuation spectrum, generally, are book value (heavy science, low art) and market value (light science, high art). Neither is a particularly satisfactory way to measure a business from the owner vision perspective.

Book value, that line on the balance sheet called "shareholders equity" or "owners equity," carries a lot of "generally accepted accounting principles" baggage (e.g., depreciation and at-cost value) that can often lead to significantly misstated "investment" value. Market value estimates, unless there is, in fact, a willing buyer offering real cash for the business, are frequently matters of semi-supported opinion, themselves clouded by "noise." Even an actual offer at a specific price may not accurately reflect the investment value of the business to the current owners. A buyer might, for example, offer far more than a business is worth based solely on assets or profitability because the buyer has an unique, or strategic objective. Eliminating a competitor, for example, can often be worth a premium, a component that would not be considered by current owners evaluating their own investment.

Valuation for the purposes of defining owner value doesn't have to follow all the rigor and justification required of formal valuations. Owners primarily need to agree among themselves as to what they define as value. They can use as much rigor as they wish, just as long as they agree the method is sensible and the resulting value acceptable.

The process is seldom excessively complex. My experience has been that, usually, some variation on either adjusted book value or capitalization of earnings, or a combination of the two, is selected by shareholders trying to define the value of their business. These can often be done on flip charts or small spreadsheets, but simplicity shouldn't imply the results are trivial. The definition, itself, is critical to the whole process of building value. The thought process involved can teach owners (as well as managers and prospective owners) a lot about the nature of their investment.

While each business will go about this exercise in its own unique way through shareholder/advisor discussions, some rule of thumb questions generally apply:

- *What adjustments to book equity are necessary to better define the actual value of our net investment?* Do we, for example, have two different kinds of investments, operating and nonoperating? Have we "parked" capital in land that we expect to become valuable in the future, but is not being used today? If so, we may want to apply differing return criteria on the two asset classes. Do we have liabilities on the books (e.g., loans from shareholders) that are really never to be repaid? If so, they really represent distributed profits, not debt.

- *What is the long-term earning power of this business?* This is an estimate, of course, but competent managers (and their advisors) do it all the time when preparing annual budgets. With a few more extrapolations and more aggressive prescience, it's usually possible to project an agreed-upon future earnings stream. Given that cash flow is one of the key "returns" for investors in operating businesses, projecting earnings streams is an important study to undertake. It can also be a critical component in determining value if the owners decide a capitalization of earnings approach is appropriate.

- *What is the appropriate rate for capitalizing our earnings to determine a value?* With earnings defined, it is possible to analyze the value of the business, particularly relative to risk, to see what underlying value would make our earning stream attractive.

Let's say, for example, that we had an investment that

generated annual earnings of $65,000. Let's say, further, that our investment carries virtually no risk. How could we determine the value of that investment? The best way would be to compare it with other risk-free investments of known value and return, most typically, the average yield to maturity on long-term Treasury Bonds (which the Federal Reserve estimates at about 6.5%).

To get a $65,000 annual return on a Treasury Bond, on that assumption, we'd have to invest $1 million, or about 15.5 times expected earnings. That's a lot of investment for a relatively low return, but, remember, there's no risk. The more risk involved, clearly, the greater the potential return we'd demand, or conversely, the less we'd be willing to invest to achieve a specific dollar amount as return.

Let's say that $65,000 was generated by a business in a volatile industry with a limited product line and a high regulatory risk. Here we might add "risk premiums" to that risk-free 6.5%. We could first add a risk premium of 7%, because that's what investors in large publicly traded stock have earned over Treasury rates since 1926. We could further add another premium of 5.2% because this company is small and that's how much better investors in "micro-cap" companies have done over "large-cap" investors over the same period.[1]

On this basis, the required return rate has increased from the risk-free base rate of 6.5% to 18.7%. We would be willing to risk less (in this case, $348,000) to get the same $65,000 return. Thus, the cap rate of this business would be approximately 5.5 times earnings (versus the

---

[1] These premiums were derived from Ibbotson and Associates, *Stocks, Bonds, Bills and Inflation, 1996 Yearbook.*

15.5 risk-free rate). The higher the risk, the lower the multiple applied to earnings to estimate underlying value. In other words, the riskier the business is, the more earnings expected for a given investment.

There are other important factors to consider. If the company's earnings are growing at a significant rate, we could consider that growth as part of the return, and deduct it from the required premium. If the company is closely held and has a lot of unique risk factors, we might increase the premium.

- *Should we use a combination of equity and capitalization of earnings to determine the value of our investment?* This judgment is made by analyzing the relative importance of assets and earnings in our sense of business value. Agricultural businesses, for example, often are heavily asset-based and generate relatively lower cash earnings than other manufacturing businesses. Service businesses, on the other hand, can have a relatively low asset value but relatively high earnings. Depending on the business, a weighting of the two approaches (e.g., 65% adjusted book value, 35% capitalized earnings) could give a more appropriate and, hence, *more likely to be accepted by all owners,* definition of value.

The answers to the above questions (more accurately the discussions leading to those answers), are essential to the process of setting investment strategy and to managing owner value. Without them, it's difficult even to know for sure if the owners want to (or reasonably, should) continue investing in the business.

Without this analysis, the shareholders can easily divide into various factions, some happy with the return, some unhappy, others generally ignorant of the whole issue. Risk and opportunity will tangle hopelessly with each other in owner discussions, and decisions increasingly will be made by default, by powerful interest groups, or not at all.

Independent of the internecine conflicts and Byzantine politics that can result among the owners because of a failure to set an investment strategy, there is another problem that results in further erosion of owner value: employees are very sensitive to confusion at the owner level, and can easily become confused and demoralized themselves.

DEVELOPING THE INVESTMENT STRATEGY

Agreeing on a set of targets or mutually agreed upon goals for a closely held business is probably the most difficult strategic decision that business owners have to make.

The "owner value management process" I've been describing and discussing throughout this book lists the investment strategy as logically prior to all other questions and decisions. That's appropriate…from a logical point of view.

Practically, it's very difficult to define a closely held business investment strategy in a vacuum. Publicly held corporations find it relatively easy to define return on investment. Standards for what is and is not sufficient return are determined by objective market forces for the IBMs and EXXONs of the world.

Private businesses are forced into much more dynamic and much less objective definitions of "good" investment performance. Owners of closely held companies have more control over that definition than shareholders of public companies. Components of private business value, particularly in family companies, tend to get fuzzy around the edges, as I discussed earlier, and can include nonfinancial considerations like career opportunity for owners and community name recognition.

Given all that, definition of an investment strategy — the statement of what we, the owners as a group, expect from our business

— is a somewhat fluid process. The definition evolves through analysis, goal-setting, budgeting, action, measurement, and review. As time goes by, owners, board, and management become more comfortable with and confident in the investment strategy.

We must begin somewhere, though, and the best way to do that is to define a set of basic investment strategy components. My clients and I have found the following to be a useful list:

- *Minimum return on investment*[2]. This is generally the easiest component of investment strategy to define, since it represents a return level equivalent to what the owners could get through readily available and low-risk alternative investments. An example minimum ROI target would be the typical return on a portfolio of large capitalization stocks. This number often functions in the compensation system in defining a return level below which no management incentive bonuses are paid.

- *Target return on investment*. Target ROI is more difficult to determine, including as it must considerations of the inherent risk in the business, the aggressiveness of the business strategy, and the psychology of the owners. Also, different components of the business could easily be expected to generate different target returns. Typically, Target ROI evolves through analysis of historic returns and owner comfort with those, comparison to industry benchmarks, and expectations of growth (investment in which can depress ROI in the short term).

- *Growth (reinvestment) rate*. It's a truism that nothing

---

[2] *Return on investment* (or "return on equity") is basically a ratio of the free cash flow from earnings available to common shareholders (numerator) to the owners' equity in the business (denominator). It is a product of profit margin, asset turnover, and leverage, the principal components of the income statement and balance sheet.

generates cash like a declining business — for a while.
Growth is essential to managing value. That growth
must either occur within the business, or outside the
business after the cash has been distributed to the
owners. This is why a definition of expected or desired
growth rate is so important to the investment strategy.
It basically is a statement by the owners as to what
extent they plan to keep their cash in the business or take
it out. There are a number of ways to express this
component. It can be the rate of increase in owner
equity, year to year. It can be stated simply as a projected growth in sales volume at a set margin. In some
cases (typically Subchapter S corporations), it's defined as a "reinvestment policy," which defines a cap on
profit distributions to owners (e.g., only the tax liability
is distributed in cash, the rest remains in the business).

- *Risk tolerance*. This might seem like a soft, indefinable
  quantity, but it can be captured in many cases through
  definition of a target financial leverage, or debt-to-
  equity ratio. In general, the less uncertainty the owners
  perceive in the marketplace, the more leverage they're
  willing to tolerate. Uncertainty is a combined function
  of external threats and internal confidence, and when
  owners agree on target leverage levels, they are really
  forced to agree upon their perceived level of tolerable
  risk.

Clearly, every organization, every set of owners, is going to
approach the investment strategy differently. Depending on the level
of financial sophistication of the owners, the depth of performance
and benchmark data available, and the power of the financial accounting system, this strategy can be complex or simple.

Level of complexity is not so important as actual existence of
a strategy in the first place. A simple statement of the above targets,
based mostly on history, can be a good beginning point.

For example:

X Company Investment Strategy

The owners of X Company expect a <u>minimum annual ROI of 14%</u> on combined operations, and believe that the company should be able to provide a rolling five-year average <u>target return of 25%</u>. We expect to <u>grow shareholder equity by at least 15% per year</u>, maintaining an <u>average leverage of .9/1</u>, and will <u>reinvest earnings as necessary</u> assuming achievement of the above targets.

This is a simple statement, but its ramifications can and should be profound. From it, the board can make decisions as to capital structure, acquisitions/divestitures, management performance goals and compensation design. The management team will have clear objectives to plug into their planning process and will know where and how their incentives are determined. Everyone will know, too, just how committed the owners are to growth, and what they are willing to risk to achieve it.

Remember, though, that this is a strategy, not a law of the universe. It can, should, and will evolve over time to fit changing circumstances and a changing owner group.

Dynamic though it may be, however, it is the fulcrum around which the stakeholders in the business will move the world.

6: Structure, "Strategic" Compensation, and Planning

Jeff even surprised himself when he slammed his fist on his desk. Two of the secretaries outside his office looked up, surprised, at the sound, then looked away quickly, embarrassed, when they caught the CFO's ungentle eye.

He's going to raid the line until we lose the bank, Jeff was thinking, as he mopped up spilled coffee with a tissue. *I worked for months on that bank, and when they see what he's doing, they're going to flip!*

This was the third time in the quarter that Mort Spencer, the owner of the business, had demanded cash, and Jeff had to use the line of credit to cover it. Again.

It's bad enough we're paying "consulting" fees to Mort's kids and an inflated salary to him, Jeff thought. *At least those expenses were in the budget. Now he expects our cash flow to carry his real estate hobby.*

The cash went out as "loans to shareholders," and (probably) would be repaid, but cash was cash. They were at the low point in the budget cycle and Jeff was pedaling furiously like a high-wire unicyclist to keep to the cash projections.

Next thing he'll want, Jeff grumbled to himself, *is more salary to cover the loan repayments. With that goes the bank line, the profits, and the bonus pool Mort so generously created last year.*

Jeff remembered how hopeful he felt when Mort set up the bonus program that essentially had no upper end. It shared a piece of the business, in a sense, something Mort didn't have to do.

Maybe I was just too stupid to realize, Jeff decided, as he called up his draft résumé, *that it doesn't matter how big the pool can get if there's always a leak in the bottom.*

Are closely held businesses run for profit? You guessed right. It depends...on what you mean by "profit."

Is that new branch office at Aspen a business expense — or is it "profit"? It depends, actually, on whether you're more likely to be selling ski equipment, or using it.

What about the company maintenance crew that keeps the shrubs trimmed and the garage painted at the house? That depends a lot on the size of the home office and, maybe, finding a way to get the neighborhood zoned commercial.

Then there's that corporate aircraft, membership in YPO, the country club dues, attendance at the Soda Straw Association meeting in Cancun. Business expenses? Profit? Depends.

Truth is, it's not smart to show too much accounting profit. That gets taxed. Business "expenses" don't. It actually makes more sense to break even, higher and higher, every year.

Or so it seems...

I once worked with a furniture retailer in the Southwest who had a unique approach to blurring this line between expense and profit. When Grandpa and Grandma founded the company, they realized furniture inventory could either sit in the warehouse or in their house. So, what the heck, they figured, use the house.

Of course, that filled their rooms, leaving no space for them to buy their own furniture. But, shucks, what was a little sacrifice?

Their pseudo-warehouse space increased proportionately with employment of their five children. Same reasoning, now becoming a family tradition.

By the time I met them, some members of the third generation were involved and others were considering the possibility. Predictably, they all wanted their piece of the tradition. This would've been fine, except the business was growing to where it needed some furniture actually *in the warehouse.*

Tension was getting thick. The most recent family hires were getting less "warehouse" furniture than their older cousins, who, in turn, were reacting like Social Security recipients: *We got ours. You might not. Way it goes.*

And so it *usually* goes. Another pre-tax "perk" that was a reasonable idea 50 years before, was beginning to chill a family's soup.

Compensation in the closely held business so often is more related to loopholes and tax codes than performance or owner value. In fact, compensation is often the primary means of delivering owner value, dividends appearing as padded salaries, unearned bonuses, and genetically determined perquisites.

All this may be fine in companies where the owners are the only key managers, or where the investment strategy is to milk the asset. For those owners who have developed a vision aimed at the ultimate legacy of preserving owner value long-term, this sort of "compensation abuse" leaves the dreamland of benefit and enters the nightmare of addiction.

If our goal is to preserve owner value in a growing business, our management team must be pointed in that direction.

To do this effectively requires the proper structure, as well as a management compensation system that is pointed more toward building owner value than distributing it pre-tax. These are key elements of the second box in the owner value management process.

DEFINING THE STRUCTURE

Assuming that the decision about maintaining ownership is made in the affirmative, and, further, assuming that the owners have set an investment strategy, the value management process should naturally proceed to the board or *structure* level. This is the level where, in theory, the "directors" do their job.

Two fundamental issues are addressed at this level (*Figure 6-1*):

1) What is the best business and organizational structure for meeting the goals of the owners?

2) What are the most appropriate performance targets and related compensation system for the management team?

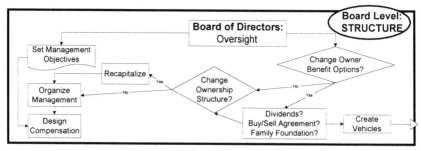

Figure 6-1: Boards are generally charged with the responsibility for assuring that the organization is structured properly, the right management is in place, and the compensation program points managers toward achieving the owner vision defined in the investment strategy. The "board" can be a real board, an advisory board, or a group of committed owners — in this sense, action is more important than form.

Usually, the two key questions above are skipped entirely, principally because the "board of directors" doesn't really exist. It's only a fantasy creature brought to life by the bylaws. The typical closely held business board has no reality or function beyond providing a header line for dusty boilerplate minutes of meetings that never get held.

Now, it's true that many businesses do quite well without a functioning board of directors, and not every company needs one. The point here is not to imply that boards are panaceas. To expect that of a formal board would be unrealistic and considerably naïve. In fact, in some ways, installing a functioning board too soon can be potentially destructive to entrepreneurial success (*Appendix A-9*).

But this is not a book about *entrepreneurial success* — creating a successful business. It is about managing the value of an existing successful business for the long term. And for *that* purpose, a body that provides the oversight functions of a board — whether it is an advisory board or even a committed group of owners — *is* essential. (See *Chapter 4* for a discussion of advisory board roles in this capacity.)

Whatever form the oversight body takes, the questions of structure and goals/compensation are prime responsibilities. They have differing urgencies, however.

Structure is, basically, an *ad hoc* issue. It arises periodically with changes in growth rate and profit, ownership composition, and the tax laws. Few companies change their capital structure regularly. Divestitures and acquisitions aren't regular agenda items in most companies.

I won't deal with structure questions in this book precisely because they are so situational and unique to specific businesses. It *is* important, however, to remember that the structure should at least be reviewed regularly, and when changes are required, they should be implemented as needed. This is a responsibility the "board" cannot ignore. It just isn't a continuing agenda item.

On the other hand, owner benefit procedures usually stay in place for years. Therefore, a much more regular and urgent review item for the board is the whole area of management performance and compensation. How goals are set and measured, how people are rewarded, and for what, are critical factors in managing owner value; they have impact almost daily.

Before we look at how things should be, however, it's necessary to look at *today* to understand and fix the way things are now.

TAKING THE "CURE" FOR PERK ADDICTION

The first step in managing compensation strategically is understanding how it can be abused. I don't need to recite the book on taxation. Most business owners know very well what we're talking about here. For many, tax avoidance grows into a profitable, almost mesmerizing hobby. It can be challenging, after all, and absorbing — a serious game, played for real dollars by people who have a lot at stake. Nothing illegal. Just a little sleight of hand and few matters of interpretation.

I've seen businesses support flying hobbies, strings of show horses, race cars, art collections, all sorts of defensible "expenses," each of which enhances the life-style of the owners, is free of personal tax, and is deductible by the business. If I've seen a lot of it, you can be sure the IRS has seen much, much more.

No big flap. Who's better at it than politicians, even some presidents? This is, after all, a nation that grew out of deep agricultural roots, and who's better than the American farmer at maintaining a life-style on seemingly no cash income at all?

These business owners were simply taking one of the few tax advantages available through their business, a little economic benefit to help offset the heavy combined corporate and personal tax bite.

The benefits of overhead expense "dividends" are obvious to all of us. Many companies survive them very well, indeed. But these survivors remind me of the panel cartoon depicting a king with his son. *"If you're very, very careful, Son,"* the king is saying, *"absolute power corrupts only a little bit."*

I'm not talking about a moral issue. It's more a practical business problem of confused business goals, conflicting policies, and corroded compensation standards.

Using pre-tax dollars for personal benefit is what I call "perk addiction." It's like taking mild "recreational" drugs. In theory, the behavior can seem innocuous. In practice, it too often can develop into financial substance abuse, damaging businesses, fraying business relationships, demotivating employees, and even destroying families.

True, the alternative — playing it straight above the bottom line — has a distinct disadvantage: we pay more in taxes. But the benefits of "going straight" can be immense. We can then set real expense and profit targets for the managers. We can use our accounting system for what it was designed — management — rather than to confuse prying eyes. We can show our financial results to the people who need to see them. We can base a compensation system on business performance without our key people resenting how the owners are depressing profits.

Perhaps most importantly, we can begin to separate personal and family needs from business needs, making it even more clear to everybody involved that the real financial future lies in a growing, profitable business, not in a pre-tax benefit system.

For the furniture retailer, the symptoms of abuse were clear: hiding new furniture pieces from other family members, periodic amnesia about whole rooms of furniture, and putting "my rightful share" ahead of family and business.

Fortunately, the addiction was recognized for what it was before the situation had deteriorated beyond recall. Once recognized, it was simply stopped. Cold turkey. Oh, they came close to falling off the wagon a number of times, but they held on. And survived.

It's our decision, of course. We can play with pre-tax dollars if we choose, but we'd better respect their power to destroy. At the very least, we should keep our eyes out for the signs of addiction.

When they come, common sense says bite the bullet, pay a little more tax, and run the business clean and straight, like a real business rather than a personal tax shelter.

The major benefit that comes from eliminating perk addiction, I've found, is more effective management. "Going straight" allows the company to actually use compensation as a strategic variable, a powerful driver of results-oriented management.

FOCUSING ON VALUE: "STRATEGIC" COMPENSATION

Before discussing the actual procedure for designing and implementing a "strategic" compensation system, we should consider the following assumptions that underlie (or *should* underlie) compensation system design:

- **Owner benefit logically precedes employee benefit.** Key employees should produce value for the owners of the business before benefiting from incentive or equity compensation. Without investors willing to support a business with capital, there would be no employment.

- **Compensation is a "compass," not an energizer**. Responsibility, commitment, and enthusiasm are functions of personality and working conditions and are usually only *negatively* affected by inadequate or poorly designed compensation.

  It was Frederick Herzberg who first made the common sense observation[1] that pay is less an energizer of people than it is a tool for encouraging *existing* energy to work in the employer's benefit. He believed that the factors that produce job satisfaction are separate and distinct from factors that produce job dissatisfaction. Pay people too little, for example, and they will become dissatisfied. Pay them "enough" and they will not become satisfied. They simply will be *not dissatisfied*.

  There have been many studies over the years that show most people place money far behind quality of work, variety, and co-workers in evaluating their jobs. More important, common sense and experience teach seasoned managers that focusing people on money can *distract* them from other goals, *including the business*

---

[1] Herzberg, Frederick. "One More Time: How Do You Motivate Employees?" *Harvard Business Review:* January-February, 1968, pp. 13-22.

goals we want them to pursue.

One difficult lesson experience teaches is that people who are irresponsible and/or lazy are unlikely to be changed solely by the promise of more money. If anything, the very traits we're trying to change are *encouraged* by overcompensation. Thus, when compensating key managers in the closely held business, we should begin by assembling responsible and capable people on the team. Our strategic compensation system is based on the assumption that we are employing such managers. Those who are otherwise should be "encouraged" to seek employment elsewhere.

Compensation, seen in this light, is not an energizer. Properly designed, it can instead be a powerful tool for freeing internally motivated (call it "responsible" if you wish) employees to focus on actions and results important to their employers. Compensation, in other words, is much more effective when used as a compass than as a kick in the posterior. *This is a critically important point to understand in designing compensation that focuses employees on building owner value.*

A well-designed ("strategic") compensation plan (via base salary, incentives and/or equity participation) will (1) allow employees to think of things other than money and (2) will serve as a tool to encourage employee "focus" or concentration of effort toward owner value. Our design should, therefore, be both generous and highly directive (i.e., goal-oriented).

- **Incentive should "point" toward owner value.** The key purpose of compensation should be to drive company objectives, true, but principally *to encourage achievement of the investment strategy.* For example:

Increasing Cash Flow (e.g., 20% annual growth).

Significant return on invested capital or ROIC (e.g., 12% annual).

Note: There are a number of possible ways to define "invested capital," which is another way of describing "owner value." We could, for example, develop a formula that proportionately weights different "return" measures in order to smooth or balance unusual events, i.e.:

A five to seven times multiple of average cash flows (before distribution to shareholders) over five years (weighting factor: 50%), combined with

Pre-distribution book value (25%), combined with

Most recent market valuation (25%).

- **Incentive should be based on *both* organizational and individual goals.** While individual performance is important and should be recognized, owner value is enhanced primarily through *organizational* not *individual* success. Incentive determined solely on individual goals/performance can inhibit both teamwork and cooperation.

Strategic compensation plans accomplish the above objectives through careful and value-related design of three components of pay: the base salary, the incentive bonus, and long-term growth participation.

For What I Know: The Hygienic Base

As compensation iconoclast, Alfie Cohn, put it:[2] "Pay people well, pay them fairly — and then do everything you can to take their minds off of money."

Typically, base salary is the fixed portion of a manager's

---

[2] Kohn, Alfie. "Why Incentives Fail." *CFO:* September 1994, pp. 15-16.

income and does not vary with company or individual performance. It is a recognition of a manager's basic economic value and the economic value of the job to the company. Since this is an employment market issue, benchmarking and other analysis of whether a given base is adequate for a given experience/skill level, competitive in the region, industry, etc., and affordable to the company are necessary and appropriate.

What is *not* appropriate, however, is using base salary as a reward. Since a base is fixed, rewarding exceptional performance (which is not fixed) through a raise is illogical. Further, given the prudent objective of controlling fixed costs in any business, salary "inflation" is something any owner wants to avoid.

The most sensible way to manage base salaries for key managers is to allow for increases only under the following conditions:

- *Increase in the general cost of living — allowing base salary increases tied to positive changes in the cost-of-living indices.* Dissatisfaction is a predictable result of salary decreases, whether caused by an actual cut or eroded by inflation.

- *Merit increases to gradually increase base for key managers who are substantially under market value.* An "underpaid" key employee is an open invitation to a recruiter.

- *Significant increase in responsibility level.* This is simply recognizing the higher economic value of the new job to the company.

There are many companies that still vary raises in salary, or even *hourly* pay, according the kind of year they had, but this is counterproductive. In Herzberg's words: "Have [spiraling wages] motivated people? Yes, to seek the next wage increase."

For What I Do: Capped and Uncapped "Incentive" Systems

If people aren't motivated by money, why even consider using a bonus or incentive system? Because, while people may not be *driven* by cash reward, they certainly do take money very, very seriously. This makes the "bonus" a powerful *pointing* tool.

Navigators use a dead-reckoning (DR) track on their chart in order to correct course after taking an actual "fix" to make sure the ship is always on the most direct route to the objective. Think of the incentive program as a DR track provided to key managers, defining for them the best course to reach the company's (and the shareholders') goals. This is what I mean by "strategic compensation."

There are two alternative philosophies of incentive design: one "strategic," the other more common, but less strategic in nature. The more strategic approach, an **"uncapped"** incentive, uses an incentive pool that is *return on investment-based and, thus, inherently lacks a predefined upper limit.* Less strategic (but strategically salvageable through careful design) is the **"capped"** incentive approach which generally defines an incentive pool which is *fixed as a percentage of base salary, although it may vary with individual performance.*

The Uncapped (Strategic) Incentive

In an uncapped, or profit-based approach, all or a portion of profits in excess of required owner return could theoretically be distributed to management (including, of course, owner-managers). A frequent concern about uncapped programs is that the managers could stand to do much better than individual owners in an exceptionally profitable year. This can be managed by using a proportional division of profits in excess of required owner return.

Incentive pool determination would proceed something like this. Assume that net income before tax (NIBT) is $x. From that we deduct the desired minimum owner return (e.g., 14% of prior year-end book value) to get $y. Of this "excess profit" amount, z% will form the incentive bonus pool for management, the remainder will go to the owners or be retained in the business. For example:

Prior year-end book value: 1,000,000
Owner minimum return
    requirement: (14%) .... (140,000)
Current year-end NIBT: 300,000
Less minimum ROI reserve: .... (140,000)
Profit excess for distribution: 160,000
Management portion (z=40%) 64,000
Shareholder Portion (1-z=60%) 96,000

Generally, *strategic* uncapped incentive programs have the following key characteristics:

- They are based on financial results rather than salary levels

- Bonus pools are funded out of current earnings

- Bonus pools are generated *after* predefined minimum shareholder returns are deducted from earnings

- Defined minimum shareholder return levels must be met by current earnings for a bonus pool to be generated in a current period

- Shareholders *and* management share earnings above the required minimum in a defined proportion

- There is no cap to bonus pool potential.

This structure is open ended, but rising profitability raises both shareholder and management boats equally.

An example of an "uncapped" incentive system used in an actual company can be found in *Appendix A-3.*

The Capped (Less Strategic) Incentive

Under a capped system, the compensation system could define a "standard" bonus as a specific percentage of base salary. A higher standard bonus can be defined for key managers, a lower "standard" for managers with less responsibility, essentially defining more than one range. This standard bonus could then be adjusted up or down by the reviewing superior during the annual review process according to each of the following two cumulative "multipliers," which could range from 0 to 1.5:

- *Organizational multiplier* — this could be set at the end of the compensation period by the Board of Directors based upon achievement of ROIC targets for the overall company, or based upon achievement of those targets for individual profit centers. Also, since teamwork is so important to management effectiveness, the organizational multiplier could be based on the success of the management team in achieving certain key goals or initiatives, or the overall achievement of strategic milestones[3] by the company or the individual profit center, as appropriate. Generally, in order for a department to achieve a 1.0 organizational multiplier (standard), shareholder value increase targets must be met **(organizational multiplier range: .5 to 1.5).**

- *Individual multiplier* — based upon specific performance of the individual and/or his profit center or responsibility area **(individual multiplier range: 0 to 1.5).**

As an alternative, a single multiplier could be used. In this approach, the "standard bonus" would automatically apply if shareholder value targets are met. Increasing that 1.0 multiplier, to any level up to the 1.5 maximum, would be discretionary. If ROIC targets are not met, the standard bonus would be decreased by the percentage target shortfall.

---

[3]"Strategic milestones" are organization-wide goals whose achievement will increase the owner value of the company, and which require the cooperation of all managers. E.g.:

Accomplishment of a specific increase in market share.

Development of a successful new product or service.

An example capped incentive bonus system can be found in *Appendix A-4.*

For What I Build: Long-Term Compensation

Incentive compensation, by its nature, is short-term in focus. This means that the "pointer" for management is also short-term in impact. Focus on immediate returns can, in fact, be detrimental to the long-term growth of shareholder value of a closely held business. Depreciation depresses earnings, for example, so one way to inflate short-term results is to minimize the capital expenditure budget, year after year. A truly strategic compensation system, therefore, must include a long-term pointer or component: growth participation in some form.

Again, I should state my "equity" component design assumptions at the outset:

- Growth participation programs generally apply only to key managers

- The objective should be to enable each participating manager to see some form of personal net worth appreciation that parallels growth in owner value

- Given the general desirability of maintaining close control, a well-designed plan avoids dilution of voting control wherever possible.

Here are the most common approaches to rewarding long-term performance:

- *Incentive Stock Options.* These are plans that provide selected key employees with the option to buy actual shares (usually nonvoting) in the company at a predetermined price.

- *Appreciation Rights or Phantom Stock Programs.* These are programs which use "shadow" (i.e., not real stock, and therefore no ownership rights) equity to give se-

105

lected key employees the status of general creditor of the company. The increase in value of appreciation rights are handled, usually, as an accrued bonus, and are tied directly to increases in the value of actual company stock. While determining the definition of "value" is problematic, it is, in general, a useful process to go through.

- *Unfunded, Non-qualified Income Deferral Plans.* These are "non-qualified" because they are provided on a discretionary basis to selected employees. They are generally exempt from ERISA requirements, require no advance approval from the IRS, and need not be funded on a current basis. Benefits are not deductible or taxable until actually paid. These plans supplement the qualified pension plan and, again, make the participating employee a general creditor of the company. Accounting treatment and the nature of the contract with the employee vary, and professional advice is essential in designing these plans.

See *Appendix A-5* for a general discussion of each long-term compensation option. Some sample phantom stock design provisions are provided in *Appendix A-6.*

SECRECY, PERKS, AND ACCOUNTING — REVISITED

While there hasn't been much discussion devoted to financial and management accounting, it should be evident that any company that plans to implement strategic compensation along lines similar to those described above must clean up — and open up — its accounting system.

The secrecy discussed in *Chapter 1*, while natural and understandable, clearly would make strategic compensation impossible. Managers cannot *manage* for results if they cannot *see* what they are managing. Further, shareholder indulgence in pre-tax dollar habits almost invariably will make it difficult to determine appropriate return on investment targets and actual ROI results.

At any rate, experience has demonstrated time and again that effective management in closely held companies arises principally from assuring that three important factors exist:

1) **Quality Employees.** Closely held companies which intend to focus on shareholder value cannot afford to become way stations for non-performers. Where loyalty issues arise, it is, in fact, usually more sensible, strategically, to provide excessive severance or maintenance packages than to allow non-performers to keep their positions in the mainstream of the management group.

2) **Clean, Functional Management and Financial Accounting.** This means designing and implementing a financial reporting system that is focused on management use rather than tax avoidance.

3) **Clear Investment Strategy, Clearly Communicated.** This is the "vision" thing, the result of shareholder effort, with key advisors, to define exactly how this investment called the closely held company should be performing, and what the owners are willing to risk to enable that performance.

Don't take this to imply that "motivational" and organizational techniques, like empowerment, team development, matrix organization, re-engineering, etc., are useless. My point is, simply, that even if we don't have the time or inclination to get into all that fancy stuff, we must, at the minimum, assure the above three fundamental elements exist in our organization. Otherwise, it's not likely that the management team will be able, effectively, to preserve owner value, long-term.

PLANNING — AND MONITORING THE PLAN

In the capstone step of the process, the management team must ask and answer the myriad questions concerning the best ways to meet the targets set for them and for the business (*Figure 6-2*). The planning process is guided by objectives and goals set for management by the "board," all drawn from the investment strategy of the owners.

Figure 6-2: Developing a business plan and putting that plan to work are the responsibilities of management. The process of managing owner value ensures that the management team knows what results they're expected to achieve, and then the process must consistently monitor their success or failure in meeting those responsibilities.

Every one of us has a number of books on the shelf covering strategy, positioning, visioning, re-engineering, you name it. The multiple facets of business planning are beyond the scope of this book.

However, over the years that I've worked as a business advisor and corporate director, I've been through planning processes with management teams many times. From those experiences, my clients and I have learned some important lessons about the real planning needs of the closely held business.

The Strategic Planning "Myth"

The most important lesson is that the benefits of formal strategic planning often don't justify the investment of time and resources. At worst, it can be a very costly mistake. As one of my more outspoken clients put it:

"Strategic planning makes no sense for a business like mine,"

108

he said, wincing a little, knowing he spoke the unspeakable.

To his surprise, I agreed.

He was the second-generation owner of a $25 million cleaning supplies manufacturing company. His growth was steady, his profitability was good, and his market share was expanding slowly — all in a market undergoing massive change. He was riding a wild wave, but managing to keep his feet on the board through a responsiveness that was almost athletic.

I compared him with a friend who'd barely survived a three-year romance with strategic planning that skirted disaster which he temporarily avoided by putting together an emergency merger with a competitor. That unfortunate fellow had been practically obsessed with strategic planning. For three years he'd kept his eyes on global objectives, writing some of the best formatted and researched business plans I'd ever seen — only to lose half (eventually *all*) of his company.

He'd spent more time planning the business than he did running it.

Most of us can think of a customer, a supplier, or a friend who got deeply involved in strategic planning and wound up sinking under the weight — too much detail, too many assumptions, just plain too much paper. A participant in a strategic planning course put it to me very well after the course was over, *"All this planning is starting to overwhelm my instinct."*

Great Tool, Wrong Application

It could. It can. It has. Strategic planning evolved as a large-organization tool and was translated for the smaller business by academicians and consultants because there were no other models to work from.

I remember taking part in a family business strategic planning seminar back in 1981. It quickly became obvious to me as the business owner-participants struggled with all the detail, that the whole process represented a significant overload for entrepreneurs. This is not a matter of managerial retardation. Successful entrepreneurs are smarter than just about anybody. The problem really is that, when asked to develop strategic plans, business owners aren't so much fish out of water as they are fish trying to swim in molasses. They're race horses who've been hobbled.

Well, we're older now. We've been through many strategic planning applications in the real, operating world of the small and mid-size company. We've seen how the process can dilute the very essence that gives the business owner his advantage.

The dirty truth of it occurred first to business owners, and has only slowly been spreading to advisors and consultants: *Strategic planning can be a cumbersome, artificial, restrictive, and numbing process.* That's what my friend learned, to his chagrin, when, one day he looked up from his planning manuals to see that his expansion had run away with his margins, and his controller had run away with the store.

The strategic planning process can translate very badly into the language of closely held companies. Private companies generally don't have the background, the staff, the money, the time, or, most importantly, the stability, for traditional (and, therefore, complex), strategic planning.

Strategic planning has its place, of course. As companies get larger, as investment levels expand, and as management teams increase in number, "strategic planning" becomes relevant and necessary. Take a look inside a DC-10 cockpit sometime. With so many crew members and so much aircraft, going so fast, there's plenty of reason for all those instruments. In a single-engine Beechcraft, however, that kind of instrumentation would be overkill — so much destabilizing dead weight.

The large organization *must* look far ahead and contemplate broad changes in course, while at the same time it can usually ignore intermittent turbulence along the way. When you're big, you can just fly through the stuff.

We smaller guys, however, have a different problem. Turbulence is the name of the game. We'd better keep our eyes outside the cockpit, because one unexpected down draft can auger us into the dirt faster than we can utter "mission statement" or spell "action plan."

Triathlon Athletes Don't Need Play Books

The problem with strategic planning, then, is not the idea behind it. Thinking long-range and managing above the grindstone are as important for the closely held business as for any organization. The problem with strategic planning is the lengthy and involved process usually associated with the concept.

That process, typically, is highly analytical — it pulls broad objectives apart, specifying, in exquisite detail, individual responsibilities, numerical goals, and time-frames. It's a process not unlike a game plan for the Super Bowl, breaking broad strategies down into individual play combinations, which are further analyzed into individual responsibilities and highly choreographed movements.

A well-played Super Bowl provides a reasonable analogy for the large-company's planning environment: lots of interchangeable players, predictable conditions, understandable rules, definable objectives.

Unfortunately, the closely held business isn't likely to be playing a Super Bowl. It's more apt to be running a triathlon. Although a long-range outlook remains important, the process of reaching goals in this event requires more integration than analysis.

The closely held business is running solo. Unlike preparation for the high-stakes *team* sports, training for individual competition usually concentrates on conditioning, practice to develop coordination and sensitivity to feedback, and, quite simply, building strength and experience. There aren't many coaches who advise runners to learn control of each muscle individually. Wisely so. There's no surer recipe for a spectacular pratfall than thinking too much about what you do well naturally — and can improve through practice. Just know the key variables, and where to look.

This is why, for most smaller and mid-sized companies, an *accurate and timely feedback system* is the closest they need to get to the kind of detailed analysis typical of strategic planning.

Focus on the Right Instruments

There are basics to business, just as there are to aviation. A pilot of any airplane, large or small, simply cannot fly without certain essential information: an artificial horizon, altitude, airspeed, fuel volume, and so forth. Similarly, every business owner, to get where he wants to go, must have timely information on sales, costs, inventory, and general market conditions (e.g., commodity prices, interest rates, RFP's). But, beyond such essentials, further analysis tends to become fluff for the smaller organization, or small-craft pilot. There's too much long-range uncertainty for "prediction," too much overall data available to synthesize into even a long-range guess.

In the smaller company, in-depth analysis quickly loses cost effectiveness. For the closely held business, protracted strategic planning can hobble instinct, confuse talent, obstruct communication, and dissipate coordination. It represents too much "getting ready to get ready" and not enough coordinated action.

Over the years, like most business owners, I've come to have a great and abiding respect for instinct. It's a kind of "strategic sense." Or maybe an evolved "genius." The most important long-range steps, then, that the business owner can take are those that *focus*, *define*, and *enable* that instinct to operate to its full capacity. Fortunately, these steps are few, and relatively easy to take.

- First, an *efficient and accurate accounting system* is required. This gives The Boss the critical information and feedback he needs to follow the terrain and avoid the mountainsides. A little "quality time" spent regularly with one's accountant can do wonders for understanding and control.

- Second, *the organization chart of the business has to be clean, clear, straightforward, and understandable.* Everyone must know who is supposed to respond to which threat or opportunity, and the organization must allow them to respond smoothly and quickly. This clarity of responsibility structure is the "conditioning" that translates mental commands into movement.

- Third, and finally, *long-range expectations have to be clearly understood and shared by all the key people in the business.* This is fundamental and, perhaps, the closest in concept to strategic planning. Unfortunately, closely held businesses have real and enduring problems with this.

Questions like these need answering: Are we in the service business long-term? Are we in the mining business long term? Are we going to grow by gaining market share from competitors, or by adding new territory/product lines? Are we a low-margin, high growth business — or a high-margin, steady growth, niche business?

Without agreement on issues like these, the internecine fighting and confusion in the cockpit leave the airplane on autopilot. You wonder who's checking the fuel gauge, not to mention who's flying the plane.

Reaching agreement is essential. But then it's critically important to get back to the business. In fact, once agreement is achieved on general direction, risk levels, growth rates, and returns, it's usually past time to get everyone's hands back on the stick, and all eyes back out of the cockpit. Continuing to focus on the flight plan won't help avoid the towering clouds outside the window.

Street fighting. Jungle warfare. Triathlons. Bush flying. Those are the models that best fit small and mid-sized companies. Certainly, we need to set the basic mission, define a few important rules of engagement, but then it's fundamental that we get on with the day-to-day job. We're really much better off leaving the global strategies — and the strategic plans — to the bigger guys. They need to concentrate on instruments and flight plans. We need to survive the scenery.

Protecting the Investment Strategy

It's the responsibility of the board to ensure that the management team orients itself, and positions the business, in ways that are appropriate to both the investment strategy and the realities of the marketplace.

That done, however, the board, and particularly the non-managing owners, should get out of the way and let the team work the plan. It's far too easy to confuse the need for oversight with an obligation to meddle in day-to-day operations.

Instead, the board should regularly review and monitor progress and operational results compared to plan. Only a few simple tools are required for this, but they are tools one seldom finds in the closely held business:

- *Operational budgets.* These are simply statements of how we plan to get where we want to go, operationally. There's nothing sacred about a budget. It has no corner on truth or predictive ability. It simply enables the board and management to see if the business is getting off the intended course, so action can be taken to correct problems.

- *Capital budgets.* These represent plans for using capital resources to make sure we meet the operational plans. Capital is precious, and usually scarce, and must be managed as carefully as the business itself.

- *Regular board and committee meetings.* It's always preferable to avoid rocks and shoals rather than to assign blame for a shipwreck. Thus, the oversight group, whoever they are, board, advisors, or owners, must have a formal process for reviewing results at least quarterly, and often more frequently.

• *Management performance reviews.* These meetings with managers close the loop between the owners' investment strategy and management compensation. They're difficult, sometimes, I know. They also take valuable time. Without reviews, however, the whole value management process is short-circuited.

Managing the "ultimate legacy" is, and will always be, a *process.* It involves owners, advisors, and managers in a dynamic relationship of definition, delegation, and oversight that can only be managed by constant attention.

Sure, the swamp is deep. The alligators are grinding and gnashing their teeth all around us. Effective operation, current profitability, and immediate response to opportunities and threats are critical to survival.

But through it all, we must remember our *purpose.* Defined and managed purpose is the rifle barrel that makes sure all the flash and energy we expend is more than just temporary noise and smoke, but, instead, actually has true aim and a positive result.

Creating and implementing a process for managing and protecting owner value, in the end, is the only real way to assure that we provide the greatest reward for ourselves and our partners — and our ultimate legacy for those who follow.

TOMORROW

7: "Strategic" Estate Planning

"What is it I have to do, Charlie, to get you to move on this plan?"

Charlie looked up from the pile of legal documents spread out on the table in front of him, and gave his old friend and attorney a small shrug.

"I'm going to sign it, Alan," Charlie said. "I just want to think about it some more."

"What's to think? We've been over it a hundred times."

"I know, but..."

"Tell me what part you don't understand. Estate plans are complicated, so maybe you don't understand something."

Charlie shuffled the documents together, and with an impatient shake of his head signaled the meeting was over.

"Just leave this with me a few days, Alan, and I'll get back to you. I promise."

Alan rolled his eyes in mock exasperation, and stood.

"Okay," he said, shaking Charlie's hand. "Don't call you; you'll call me, right?"

Charlie showed Alan out of his office, then went to the old leather chair by the window. It was a beautiful spring day, and Charlie thought wistfully of simpler times and manageable decisions.

He watched the 18-wheelers drifting in and out of the warehouse. *Dad would be dumbstruck if he saw all this.*

Charlie thought about the documents on his desk, all the trusts, insurance policies, and complex gifting procedures. He understood it all perfectly well. At bottom, it was very simple: give it all away, Charlie, as fast as you can, to the sons and daughters, nephews and nieces who will be running the company after you and your brother are gone.

Presumably, his brother was doing the same. All for the good of the families and the business.

Give it all away.

For 42 years, he and his brother worked hard precisely so they could have the "blessing" of facing this decision to pass on the company.

Give it all away...

Charlie, and thousands of other owners like him, face such dilemmas that take on privately epic proportions. They don't talk about any of it. They pretend everything is under control and they're "taking care of it."

And while they slip further into indecision and worry, their heirs grow more frustrated, their employees more anxious, their bankers, suppliers, and customers more uneasy, and their advisors more frustrated.

Many years ago, I worked with the president of a casualty insurance company, a business he owned equally with his older brother. Both men were in their sixties.

His problem was disability. It had struck the older brother a nonfatal, but devastating blow in the form of a brain aneurysm. He had survived, thanks to expert medical care, but he'd lost that special edge that made him valuable to the business.

"I know, it's like talking to a heart surgeon who chain smokes," he said to me from behind his desk. *"Believe me, the embarrassment is almost as bad as the problem.*

The embarrassment? Well, these specialists in the benefits of insurance had no insurance themselves, life or disability.

"My brother has been drawing his full salary for almost two years since his stroke," the client continued. *"I don't begrudge him that, except he's not producing any business whatsoever. Hasn't since he got sick. And lately he's been a disruption in the office.*

"I don't know what to do. He thinks he's working just as well as before. His wife says he's made a remarkable recovery, although I'm not even sure she believes it. But we can't afford to pay him anymore. It's a disaster."

He was right. It was a disaster. There wasn't much to be done, and since he couldn't afford to buy out his brother, much less continue his salary, that company was eventually sold.

We can't predict everything, good or bad, that might happen to us and those around us, but we can define probabilities. None of us is immortal. Health, while it can be impressively stable, is not indestructible.

We know this, but, in spite of that knowledge, we so often abandon common sense when it comes to protecting ourselves and our businesses from avoidable problems.

We wear seat belts in cars. We carry life preservers in boats. But we don't plan for ownership transition and personal security in the predictable events of death and disability.

Strange behavior, that. After spending a few decades on this planet, most of us can imagine many ways things could go wrong — and we do, usually at the most helpless moments, like those three a.m. "blink" sessions.

What if a key shareholder were to die tomorrow? What would happen to his/her stock or ownership interest? What would happen to his/her survivors? Is this what we want to happen?

What if disability should strike? Would there be enough income for the disabled owner? How much would the business have to pay? Would the business survive the hemorrhage? Is this what we want to happen?

What if one of the partners is ready to retire in 10 years? How will his/her ownership be transferred? How much income will be available? Is this what the other owners want to happen?

What if death costs and taxes are more than cash flow can handle? Where will the cash come from? How healthy will the business be after those costs are paid? Is this what the owners want to happen?

Surprisingly, these are relatively easy questions to answer — particularly with the help of competent advisors. We can't predict which event will actually occur, or when, but we can project what would result if any given scenario actually became reality.

In some cases, not much can be done to minimize the damage. Sometimes, we've simply waited too long, and the situation is just too far out of hand to fix.

Sometimes. But, most often, steps can be taken to protect the business and assure some security for its current and potential owners. The key to success, here, is to develop contingency plans, today, for the problems we know we're likely to face tomorrow.

If our goal is the protection and building of owner value, we *must* put common sense back into gear, and get the proper planning completed.

The operating word is *today*. It's one thing to be a business owner, 55, in good health, and planning for death or disability. It's a very much different thing to be a business owner, 70, in failing health, and planning for those same problems.

Retirement sounds easy and attractive. In actuality, it's the toughest career change most of us will have to make, one that only works out well after long preparation and planning. Time is important for many reasons. For example, gifting can only be done effectively over a period of years. Another example is insurance, which, despite our prejudice to the contrary, is often an antidote for the poisons of fate. Trouble is, insurability and premium affordability decrease almost geometrically as the years pass by.

Time. Our most precious asset. And every day we have less of it available. Worse still, we don't know *how much less.*

It's worth remembering this country wisdom:

The best time to plant an oak tree was 20 years ago.

The next best time is today.

WHY WE DON'T: THE GREAT TRANSITION MYTHS

Charlie is not going to sign Alan's carefully constructed, even somewhat brilliant plan. He's not going to sign for a lot of reasons, some buried so deeply no one will ever know them, including Charlie.

Some reasons for resistance can be predicted, however. They can even be managed in a way that can make the transition process more efficient, effective, and possibly pleasant for those affected.

To understand this, we need to explore a few myths that keep popping up as suspension-busting speed bumps on the road to ownership protection and transition plans:

Myth: You must give it all away

Charlie is staring out the window, with the estate plan unsigned and unexecuted, because its fundamental purpose is unacceptable to him. He has spent his life building, and now, just when he thinks he's about ready to start enjoying what he built, he's presented with a plan that assures it will be ripped from his hands.

That's what the experts seem to be saying: "Get it out of your estate, Charlie."

But I just got it IN!

This fundamental conflict of purpose is almost always unnecessary. There are many technical approaches available to move value and keep control (or vice versa), but since the advisors are usually told only, *"find some way to move this thing to the next generation without any tax liabilities,"* they assume that the current owners do, in fact, *want* to give it all away.

Advisors can generally handle either goal. There are ways,

through various classes of stock and specific kinds of trusts and partnerships, to, in essence, give it away without giving it away.

If only Charlie had the courage to admit his desire to hold on, or his attorney had the sensitivity to ask whether he really wanted to give it up, both would realize the plan on Charlie's desk will never be signed because it doesn't meet Charlie's needs or fit *all* of his goals.

Myth: Management succession requires ownership transfer

On the surface, it seems obvious that a business owner who wants to transfer management responsibility to his eventual successors must also give them the same kind of control over the business that he enjoyed during his reign. How else can they continue to build on his entrepreneurial successes?

This puts the owning generation in a dilemma, however. If the successor-managers aren't ready to take full control, the present owners have to maintain that control…yet, the successors can't prove they're ready to take control unless it's given to them! What's the answer? Typically: do nothing.

Rethinking this myth, we can take this approach: why not separate the issues of management authority and ownership control altogether? With the proper business and ownership structures, it is, in fact, possible to allow management the authority it needs to achieve defined targets, while reserving for others the power to make major decisions about the future of the business. This is precisely what budgets, performance targets, incentive compensation, and boards of directors are all about.

Myth: The heirs want it all now

Maybe we don't have to give them control, you might be saying to yourself, but those younger managers will be de-motivated if they don't have the power of ownership. Sounds logical, but experience has shown something quite different.

What successor managers and heirs want is not immediate

control or possession. Oh, sure, it would be nice, but it's not necessary as long as they have a clear understanding of how control and benefit will be distributed in the future, along with solid assurance that the owner value will be wisely and prudently administered in the meantime. If a lot of time will pass before the transfer occurs, they want to know that, somehow, they are building value for themselves in the interim (e.g., through deferred compensation, phantom stock, etc.).

Despite all the jokes about silver spoons, most of the heirs I have met fully appreciate the nature of the legacy their forebears have built for them. They know, too, who built it, who took minimum return over so many years, and who wants to take benefit today.

At the same time, however, the heirs also realize that it is unwise for them to simply drift along and wait for something to happen. Time is precious to everyone, and the next generation is very interested in knowing that they are not wasting theirs on vague promises with no foundation and diminishing return.

Myth: Minority ownership is worthless

This is heard so many times in so many variations that it's hard to consider objectively. After all, what possible value does minority ownership in a closely held business have, particularly for someone who doesn't work in the business and can't take benefit in the form of salary and perks?

Besides, everyone has heard more than one story about disgruntled outside shareholders and the grief they can cause.

The logical conclusion? Make sure that non-involved heirs get assets other than stock. Give them cash, trusts, the lodge in New Hampshire, the family antiques, but never, ever, give them a piece of the business.

That's what logic says. What about the heart? Is it possible that current owners, like Charlie, for example, hesitate to follow this sort of "logical" recommendation from their professionals because it sounds a lot like disinheritance?

Here's what Charlie could be thinking as he stares out his window:

That plan leaves Margie no stock in the business. It's simpler, I know. It'll make life easier for Johnny and his cousins who'll be building the company. That way, she wouldn't have to depend on them.

I know. I know. But Dad built this for me and my brother. We built it for our kids. Am I supposed to now disinherit my grandchildren, Margie's kids? Exclude them from the business? How can I do that?

Logic and the heart can conflict mightily, and the result of that conflict can be a seemingly inexplicable resistance to sign and execute a perfectly logical estate plan.

Fortunately, if a closely held business is structured around the principals discussed in this book, and the focus of owners, directors, and managers is kept firmly on defining, preserving, building, and distributing owner value in the long term, outside minority ownership can, in fact, be a valuable thing — a productive investment — without being a drag on the active owners.

One other point: the existence of outside minority owners can be a wonderful periodic wake-up call for inside owners, who can too easily get distracted by operational pressures, and forget to consider owner value.

Myth: In-laws aren't family

The following conversation stands out very firmly in my memory whenever the subject of "in-laws" comes up:

Carl was upset. I remember staring, amazed, at the plastic swizzle stick he'd just reduced to free molecules, before looking up again to his reddened face.

"She's hurting my wife, Doc," he said. "I just won't have that..."

"She," in this case, was his daughter-in-law, Dana, the wife of his successor-son, who was the sole heir to the family car dealership.

"Do you really believe it's deliberate, Carl?" I asked.

"I didn't before, but now...I don't know. She can't just 'accidentally' show up hours late for every family function. How could she not know it's an insult to sit with John and me, while Mary's out in the kitchen cleaning up after dinner?

"And now John says he's going to try going home earlier, so he can spend more time with Dana. That's not his idea. It's hers.

"I won't put up with it, Doc. This business built their house, feeds them, and clothes their kids. It's not just some hobby that gets in the way of wedded bliss!"

Fortunately, the arrival of our steaks headed off Carl's oncoming cardiac arrest, letting us get back to the subject later, after Carl had calmed down.

For Carl, as for many other business owners, the appearance of sons- or daughters-in-law signals the arrival of a perpetual hurricane season. Somehow, everything changes. Cooperative, hard-working successors grow evasive and uncooperative. Comfortable family dinners evolve into increasingly cool and emotion-laden tests of endurance.

Under these new pressures, the business can unexpectedly change from golden goose to camel in the family tent.

Forget for a moment the in-laws' influence with the successors and other owners. Just ask yourself whether your sons-in-law, daughters-in-law and siblings-in-law have an interest in the future of the business. Might they be chewing over questions like: "Is it profitable?" "Where is it going?" "How will the ownership be distributed?" "Who will be the next president?"

Are these reasonable questions? Sure. Do these people have good reason to ask them? Probably. Is it any of their business? Well...this is the tough part. "Maybe," you're probably saying. "It depends."

In reality, it doesn't *depend* at all. The family business is a wagon train through hostile territory, and everyone on that train, whether he or she owns the wagons and horses or not, is very interested in the route, protection along it, the destination, and the reason why the trip is being taken in the first place.

Just as the "wagon master" has a right to ask everyone to take part in the risk and the effort, in return, everyone who joins the trek has a right to be part of the dream.

You might be resisting this idea, and if you are, you're definitely not alone. The resistance comes with all sorts of reasons, usually taking some form of "We don't need in-laws telling us how to run our business."

The objection is valid, as far as it goes.

I'm not suggesting getting the in-laws involved in the operation of the business. Let the scouts continue to find the trails. Let the wagon master decide which trails to take, how to manage defense, and how to control the supplies. Let the "teamsters" drive the wagons.

But we must remember this. If the trail turns bad, or the supplies run out, or a wagon breaks, or an opportunity requires risking the whole venture — every owner group will need the support of their spouses. And that support will depend on how well they've been brought into the decision-making process from the beginning.

This is why the benefits of inviting owner spouses (actual and potential) to every owner meeting far outweighs the risks.

Unless the in-laws are included in the owners' decision-making processes in a constructive and positive way, they will almost inevitably resist many of the decisions that are made. This resistance will lead to conflict behind the heirs' or partners' closed doors.

And this conflict will vastly confuse and derail any potential for efficient ownership protection or estate planning.

HOW WE SHOULD: SETTING "STRATEGIC" PRIORITIES

The Priority Diagram below *(Figure 7-1)* lays out a more rational and effective order of attack for planning effective ownership protection and transition. Note that tax-saving strategies, rather than getting either first or last priority, should be considered a key planning variable at *all* levels — *key*, but not paramount.

The priorities are important for a number of reasons, most important of which is that they focus planning on issues in the order they will most probably become problems. Almost as important, this kind of explicit statement of relative importance sends a clear message

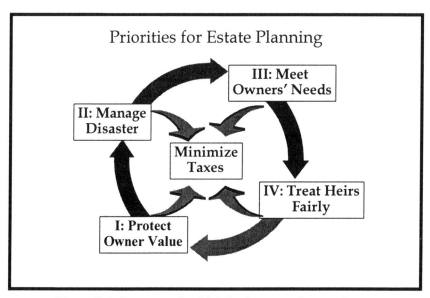

Figure 7-1: Tax issues shouldn't be the major drivers of estate planning, or even the management of ownership, in general. The fundamental goal is to protect value, while doing as much as possible to meet various needs of the owners, the heirs, and the business — always with one eye closely focused on taxes.

129

to the professional advisor team as to where they should focus attention.

Remember that the goal of protecting ownership assets and planning their transfer is most often continuity, not the saving of taxes nor even the manipulation of power. While the purity of motives might change as future generations get involved with the business, continuity is usually the goal of the owner(s) as he or they do their crystal ball gazing.

Since every plan usually sets the tone for the future, the quality of that plan has a lot to do with what future generations do. Quality, in turn, depends on getting the priorities right and developing the right plan components at the right time.

Let's examine the priorities in turn.

Priority #1: Protect Owner Value

Without foresight and careful planning, all sorts of decisions can ultimately decrease owner value. Generation skipping, for instance, while useful for tax planning purposes, can (if improperly designed) result in a loss or dilution of control. Setting value artificially low in a buy/sell agreement in order to reduce estate taxes is another example where owner value could be reduced with undesirable results for owners who happen to keep on living.

These are just two illustrations of the important priority to protect owner value. It is, perhaps, the easiest priority to understand, but the most difficult to achieve. It is a consideration to keep in mind always.

Think of it as a template against which every other decision is made: *whatever problems this might solve or whomever's needs it might meet, does it ultimately protect the value of our business, our assets, and our wealth?*

Priority #2: Manage Disaster

The first objective in ownership protection is to peer into the near-term future and consider what could happen to derail any long-range intentions or goals we might have for succession or ownership transition. By this, I don't mean business reversals (which we manage through tactical and long-range planning), or acts of nature, social upheaval and the like (which we either protect ourselves from through insurance or simply hope won't happen because no protection is possible).

I'm referring to such predictable, but not necessarily likely events as premature death of an owner, disability of an owner, divorce, even legal actions against a partner or owner, each of which can have a major devastating effect on the most technically tax-wise ownership plan.

We can't predict the form such disasters will take, when they will occur, or even *if* they will occur, but we can easily imagine the negative effects they could have on the business, the family, and the other owners. Planning won't help us avoid these events, but we can manage the future in ways that control their negative effects. The most common tool for this is the shareholder or buy/sell agreement.

The Buy/Sell Agreement

Buy/sell agreements (also referred to as "shareholder agreements") are instruments for covering various potential issues that can arise between individual shareholders, among shareholder groups, or between shareholders and the company.

The major objective of such agreements is to settle as many questions as possible in advance, both to control tax consequences of transactions and to help assure continuation of harmonious relationships among owners.

While the actual construction and drafting of a sound agreement is a technical process requiring the input of professional advisors, the basic considerations that go into its design are well within the capabilities of the owners to determine. In fact, developing a list of the key issues to be settled and the philosophies to be used in those settlements, is one of the best ways for partners in a business to begin planning for the future.

Consider some of the central questions that should be asked and answered in preparing to draft a shareholder agreement:

- *What are the events that will trigger the agreement, and what would we like to see happen in each event?* Typical triggering events are death, disability, termination of employment, marital status changes, retirement, and shareholder deadlocks.

- *Should purchases of stock be mandatory or optional?* This can vary with the trigger event, and whether the event is voluntary or involuntary.

- *Do we need a "cross purchase" or a "redemption" agreement?* There are tax differences to be considered here, as well as the number of owners, whether a trust or trusts are involved, and the funding available.

- *What strategic issues impact on the design of our agreement?* Long-range health of the industry, management strength, and need for flexibility are some major considerations here.

- *How will the business be valued for the purposes of this agreement?* This is often the most difficult part of the design discussions, and achieving agreement here can be the most central benefit of a finished agreement. (See *Chapter 5* for a discussion of business valuation.)

- *What sorts of benefits must be coordinated with the terms of the agreement?* All sorts of considerations arise here, from deferred compensation, through supplemental retirement plans, to consulting and perquisite agreements.

Some sample language for buy/sell or shareholder agreements

132

is included in *Appendix A-1*.

Funding

This is not a book on planning techniques or insurance products, so my remarks on funding ownership transfer will be brief.

One thing is certain, however, and that is the great likelihood that some sort of funding or protection vehicle will be necessary to ensure that provisions of a shareholder agreement will be affordable to individuals and the company. Otherwise, they are simply empty promises. This funding necessity usually, although not always, implies the need for insurance in some form.

For example, cross-purchase agreements (where a surviving owner agrees to purchase a deceased owner's equity) often require a significant amount of cash. These requirements can be self-funded, of course, but life insurance can often be a safer and more cost-effective approach. Disability is another very critical potential cash drain situation where funding through insurance could be useful.

Professional Advisors

No matter what you might think of insurance, and insurance agents, for that matter, the products available can be valid planning tools and the services provided by life underwriters can be critical to your planning success. Too many business owners have let prejudice and prior uncomfortable experience prevent them from getting the help and advice they need in this area.

The scope of shareholder agreement provisions and the complexity of interrelating them and the funding that might be required is broad. This makes it absolutely essential that you surround yourself with a *team* of the best professionals — an accountant, an attorney, and a life underwriter — that you can find, and then put that team to work helping you through both the short-term and long-term issues of ownership planning.

It's essential that these advisors work as a team. The specific and important reasons for this are discussed in the *Chapter 4* section on advisory boards.

Priority #3: Meet Owners' Needs

Once the potential impact of short-term disasters has been managed as well as possible, transition planning moves to issues of management and ownership transfer. Too often, however, this move is made in haste and often with an ill-considered emphasis on the technical, tax-saving aspects of ownership transfer.

The so-called "generation-skipping" trusts of the late 70s provide an example of how this emphasis can be ill-considered. Today, many business owners are finding themselves severely shackled by inexperienced and/or inappropriate owners to whom ownership was transferred years ago as a tax-saving strategy. My point is not to attack legitimate tax avoidance ploys. I just want to reiterate the need to establish priorities that go beyond minimizing payments to the government.

An excellent place to begin establishing these additional priorities is to look closely at the needs of the present owners *before* giving detailed thought to benefiting the next generation. Three areas of concern here:

- Control over the business and the investment it represents

- Retirement and income requirements

- Involvement in the business.

Big issues, these. They trip many a business owner and derail a large percentage of seemingly acceptable plans.

Control Issues

There is nothing in the Scriptures or natural law that mandates "giving it all away" before we leave this Earth to join the Eternal Cash Flow. Actually, among the most important benefits of wealth are influence and independence, both of which can be destroyed by premature "divestiture."

We don't like to say things like this in public, generally, but the truth is that business owners are not motivated solely by altruism. One of the great attractions of business ownership is the power and control inherent in "the vote." Especially for people who are effective, the ability to influence events is an essential feature of life.

As Charlie found out from his advisors, however, the politically correct action is to give it all away. He understands that perfectly well. He also understands why it's the "right" thing to do.

He understands, too, that of two business owners, one of whom has held onto his assets, the other of whom did the "right" thing, the former probably will be seeing more of his children and grandchildren.

This isn't cynicism. It's a realistic fear, founded in insecurity and built from observation. There are more reasons, personally, to maintain control, influence, and power than there are to give them away.

These are not issues that can be judged in terms of right or wrong. They are realities that estate and transition planning must take into account. It's not enough that the advisors or the heirs be comfortable with the plan. The current owners must be comfortable, also, and frequently this requires gradual rather than wholesale relinquishing of control over the business and the assets.

There are ways to do this without disastrous tax consequences or inevitable revolution among the next generation. Taxable equity can be moved without transferring control over key decisions or the business. Heirs can be informed, specifically, how such a plan will inevitably result in their gaining control over the business, while deferred compensation and phantom equity programs can relieve their concerns about having a bird in hand.

But these results are possible only if the current owners'

135

probable need to maintain control is given its due, and considered openly by the advisors doing the planning.

The bottom line is this: if plans are not designed with the current owners' needs in mind or if control issues are ignored, so, too, will the cleverly designed estate plan be ignored.

Charlie is likely to sit in that chair by the window for a long, long time.

Retirement Income

A good way to ruin an evening is to pull up to an exclusive restaurant, hard-to-get reservation in hand, only to discover you have no cash or credit cards. An under-funded retirement is much worse. *That* evening goes on for the rest of your life.

Although there are exceptions, in most cases retirement of an owning generation must compete for cash with capital investment in the ongoing business. Unless provision is made for both, even the best management and ownership transfer plans are headed for deep trouble.

Every situation has unique twists, but the planning model presented in *Appendix A-11* can be useful in beginning the process of balancing these competing demands in a positive way.

Disengagement from the Business

To assume that surrendering connections to the operation of the business is necessary, good for the business, or healthy for the retiree is a mistake.

Years spent successfully building a business earn one a right to maintain some influence and contact with that business. As with ownership and management transfer, potential problems can be managed by working through the planning process in a systematic way that clearly separates owner considerations from strategic issues, from operational decisions (see *Chapter 3*).

Priority #4: Treat Heirs Fairly

For a transition to work, ownership and management must be transferred in ways that minimize the potential for conflict among future generations.

The problem of equity distribution is a most agonizing one for the business owner, who, in most cases, sees his business as a legacy for his children. A legacy is something one should be able to draw benefit from forever, he thinks quite naturally, so he concludes his heirs should have the benefits of his business forever. He thereby confuses ownership with benefit — a confusion many non-involved minority shareholders are disabused of very early.

In many companies, for example, the major conflict between the owning families in future generations is a disagreement over whether to pay dividends or reinvest for expansion. One option tends to preclude the other.

Understandably, inside owners would like to see expansion. That solidifies their places in the company — and, besides, they're already taking their "dividends" out in the form of salary. But the stability of those benefits can be very fragile for them, particularly if they are minority owners with no real control over the business. The operational rug can be yanked at any time by dissenting outside partners.

Non-involved shareholder/relatives don't have a salary and very few perquisites. They often own a significant portion of a sizable company, yet, for them, there is no "benefit" at all — unless large dividends are paid, something that would turn the company into a cash (and dying?) cow.

Is this the kind of legacy Great Granddad really had in mind for his heirs?

It's important to distinguish carefully between wealth and opportunity in ownership transfer planning:

- *Wealth* is opportunity, but it's an undefined opportunity without a base.

- *Opportunity*, of the kind represented by the business, carries the promise of a fairly unlimited future at the price of a relatively limited present.

This isn't to say that wealth and opportunity should be distributed independently, but it indicates the variability and richness of options available to current owners when they design their transfer plans. Owners don't have to leave *opportunity* to everybody. That is appropriate only for those who want and can make use of it.

All this boils down to two questions:

- Is it fair for non-working family members to share equally in the equity growth spurred by the work and talent of the family managers?

- Is it fair for working family members to take benefit from salaries and perks while non-involved owners receive only paper growth?

The answer to both questions is "yes" …with conditions.

Wealth

There surely is plenty of precedent in economic history for the concept of investors benefiting from the labor of managers. A majority of business owners recognize this, and see the business they built as one of the best potential investments around. They want their heirs, *all* of their heirs, to benefit from this potential.

Two problems usually stand in the way of this goal: outside owner "meddling" with operations, and the lack of real equity "value" for the outside owners. These problems aren't inherent in minority ownership, however. They are the results of poor planning.

"Meddling" can be controlled through appropriate communication of information to the outside owners, coupled with clear and public management performance goals and measurement. Yes, it's true that increased communication of information to outside owners increases the risk that sensitive information will find its way to the outside world. But that's a *risk*, only, not a fundamental bar to communication. Business owners are used to managing risk.

Achieving equity "value," the second problem for outside minority owners, is part of the planning process, too. It can be defined, controlled, and administered through a well-designed shareholder agreement. (See *Appendix A-1.*)

Opportunity

For those family members who choose to take the risk of ownership *and* desire to work in the business, extra benefits should be available. These *opportunity* benefits can take many forms — career growth, increasing income, stock options, perquisites — and can accrue to working owners over and above the benefits they take as investors (see *Chapter 6*).

This, too, is common sense and founded on plenty of precedent. Anticipated, agreed upon, and built into the system, "opportunity benefits" can work beautifully. Again, what causes the problem here is poor planning.

Owner-managers are in a unique fiduciary position when there are non-managing owners. They are at the day-to-day controls of other peoples' investments, and have significant opportunities to manipulate expenses and investments to their own benefit at the expense of the outsiders.

Certainly, there must be a degree of trust, here, but that trust can be reinforced effectively through strong policies, open reporting systems, a rational compensation system for key management, and the involvement of trusted outsiders (e.g., a compensation committee composed entirely of trusted, mutually accepted outside directors and/or advisors).

It can be a serious mistake, on the other hand, to lose sight of

139

exactly who it is that produces business success and growth. Effective managers must be compensated for achieving goals and building wealth for the owners. *This is true whether they are owners themselves or not.*

Outside and inside owners can coexist, just as wealth and opportunity can. We have to understand the distinct nature of each, how they are independent, where they overlap, and how to apply them with wisdom.

Minimizing Taxes

You probably noticed that beating Uncle Sam at his confiscatory game is not listed in the flow of priorities. That's because it's always there, right in the center, affecting everything. (See *Figure 7-1.*)

Taxes are the root of all evil. Okay. We've said it. We all agree. Now, let's get practical.

Tax avoidance is a high-level objective in estate and transition planning, but it shouldn't stand alone an any order of priority. Tax considerations should serve, instead, as touchstones in comparing competing planning options, rather than drivers of the planning process itself. The reasons:

- *The objective of transition and estate planning is to preserve owner value — business value, asset value, personal value — not the saving of taxes.* Although significant, tax avoidance through various techniques is only one way to preserve owner value.

- *Many tax planning techniques, "erotically" attractive though they may look in a slide presentation by an out-of-town expert, can diminish and sometimes destroy value in the long term.* Talk to anyone who's been the unwitting victim of poorly planned ESOPs or inappropriately applied generation-skipping trusts.

- *Tax laws change.*

140

- *Businesses change.*

- *Personal situations change.*

Planning priorities should consider business and personal goals and needs first, then select among the alternatives for reaching those goals on the basis of tax efficiency.

Taxes *are* onerous, burdensome, confiscatory, and frustrating. Even so, they fall most heavily on those who have the most, a problem many human beings on this planet would give a precious limb or two to have.

Remember, there's an easy way to avoid paying taxes altogether. Just stop earning money.

8: Thoughts for Today's Owners

"Hal's planning on retiring, Judy," Mary told her friend in a quiet voice. "I don't know what I'm going to do."

"What's his plan?" the concerned friend asked.

"That's part of the trouble. He's got it all worked out in his head — or so he says — and I'm worried about whatever it is he's 'worked out.'"

She withdrew into silence, gazing at pedestrians strolling outside the café window, while the waiter served the coffee. Judy could tell by the distant look in Mary's eyes that she was truly worried. Hal's retirement wasn't just a passing issue.

"I know everybody retires," Mary continued after the waiter had left. "Our lawyer's telling us it's time to give the business to the kids, and I know Hal is tired of all the problems he's carried for 40 years. But when he starts talking about how much we love to travel and 'now we'll have time,' I get really worried."

"But it sounds like retirement would be good for both of you. You've always wanted to travel more, and now he *will* have the time."

Mary stared at her friend.

"He's always *hated* traveling, Judy."

With Hal, the dream is "travel." For others, it's "fishing" or "all the golf I never had a chance to play." Whatever the specifics of these sunset Valhalla's, they're usually only pipe dreams, illusions rooted in wistfulness, and driven by confusion.

That's pretty strong, I admit, but you can't spend 20-plus years working closely with business owners without developing some biases. This is one of mine.

Okay. Let's say you have a retirement "plan." You may even know that, in your case, things will be different. Fine.

It's not that golf or fishing or travel can't make for a great retirement. Many people — including business owners — retire to them successfully. The real question (and Mary had her finger right on it) is: if The Boss never found time for travel (or fishing or golf) while he was working, was it really the lack of time, or was it mainly a general lack of enthusiasm?

The answer's fairly obvious.

CONFUSING SUCCESS WITH TALENT

In order to see business transition in a context that helps us move through it, we must think clearly about this thing called "letting go." My client and friend, Will provides a good example of what I mean. I remember the conversation very clearly:

"But don't you see, Don," Will said over the cockpit intercom. "It's hard to find anybody who knows this business."

I was silent for a moment as he went into a steep bank and dropped the helicopter in for the landing. My white knuckles were absorbing most of my attention.

Will was a successful electronics distributor with a powerful weakness for rotary wings and bubble canopies. He involved himself in his hobby with the same fierce intensity he devoted to his business. But his most recent expansion — the new warehouse we were visiting that day — had taken him into uncharted territory. He was worried.

"How well do *you* understand it, Will?" I finally asked as the skids bounced on the landing pad.

We'd been discussing some major inventory and computer problems he was having, and I'd suggested that he talk to other people who'd had the problem.

Will, like so many of the business owners I've worked with over the years, believed that the uniqueness of his business made it impossible to get informed help from outsiders.

Lonely heroes that they are, entrepreneurs like Will just keep adding new burdens to their own shoulders as the business grows. Eventually, inevitably, the hero bends under the load. Some even break. Will wasn't breaking, but his shoulders were getting very near to the ground.

It's an occupational hazard, loneliness, and most successful business owners succumb to it at least once during their careers. Some never get beyond it. Truth is, to the extent that any of us are going it alone, we are confusing success with the ability to maintain and grow that success.

Fact: we build businesses on our strengths, compensating for weaknesses by hard work, fierce determination, and more hard work. This can be successful — for a while. But strength and determination can't add hours to a day, or clarity to a tired mind, or energy to a tired body. Those limits are reached long before the business reaches its limits of growth and complexity.

Will had reached those limits with his new warehouse. He knew electronics distribution, but suddenly he needed to become a materials handling expert, a telemarketing specialist, a real estate developer, and, yes, even a politician to fight with a zoning board.

"I can handle it," he told me. "Always have."

This sounds real good, until you think about it. The logic is seriously flawed. It equates "always have" with "always will."

There is an infinity of issues to decide and manage in a successful business. For each of those issues, there is usually somebody who's been there before, or who's made a study of the subject, or who knows what works and what doesn't. Sometimes, this is The Boss, but not always.

Will, for example, needed to decide how to process the greatly increased number of orders that would result from his expansion. He needed to expand his customer service department, automate the ordering process, and computerize scripts for phone sales people to handle. He also needed to negotiate the cost of a new sewer system that came at him out of the blue.

He needed help badly. Sure, he had some good people on his management staff. But they weren't hired as co-pilots. Navigators, yes. Stewards and mechanics, of course. But to none of them could Will turn and say: "Help me land this thing. I'm tired."

After a certain peak of success, we all become increasingly ineffective at what we know and do best. The reason is that we know too much. Ask yourself when you made some of the best decisions of your entire career. If you're over 50, you'll probably agree that it was back when you were too dumb and naïve to know you shouldn't do it.

What the growing business needs is a steady stream of smart, aggressive, energetic managers who, basically, don't know enough to know what they can't do.

That means that we "old goats" are between the very sharp horns of a very perplexing dilemma. We love involvement and have proven our effectiveness, yet, at the same time, we need to step aside if the next generation is ever going to make its real contribution.

The transition to the younger generation of managers is, in short, a transfer of control to committed, trained, intelligent, aggressive men and women, who are too "dumb" to know what they can't do.

Would we *really* have gone to the moon if we thought about what it *really* required?

Planning that New Career

For those of us who've done little other than work hard over the years, planning a full-bore retirement can be as much of a major mistake as hanging around, semi-retired, screwing up the business, part time.

146

Still, we're not carrion yet. We can still fog a mirror, move a stone, make a buck. The implication is that we should forget about retiring, and aim, instead, at two objectives:

A steady reduction of *risk interest* in the business.

Self-promotion to jobs *we* enjoy.

Objective 1 (which will take careful management and estate planning) meets two essential requirements.

First, it helps the current owner-manager relax and stop worrying so much about successor-manager work habits, commitment, etc. As the risk increasingly becomes theirs, it gets easier to let them do it their way. It'll never be truly "easy" to let somebody else take over our businesses, of course, but "easier" is sure better than "impossible."

Second, increasing the successor-managers' risk level is the most effective entrepreneurial training ground there is.

Objective 2 (which will require some honest self-evaluation) is aimed at allowing current owners to harvest the fruits of those 40 (or whatever) years of hard work. Three key elements are essential in meeting this objective: flexibility, independence, and significance.

Flexibility

Since there's nothing wrong with a gradual change in lifestyle, it's important to have the time and opportunity to travel, play more golf, or go fishing. Hence, the new job shouldn't be tied to the day-to-day demands of the business. "Gradualness" means that the retiree should be free to dip in and out of responsibilities that are meaningful.

This is usually what we mean when we talk about "retirement." Better terms would be "easing up" or "taking some regular time off."

Independence

The Boss hasn't worked for anybody for years, if ever. So, whatever he does now should be his to control. Sure, it sounds good to "work with the Sales Manager" or "help the Kid out," but that's about as realistic as expecting a former President of the United States to become a Cabinet officer in a new Administration.

Ignore this one at your — and everybody else's — peril. Kings don't become subjects. They become respected (we hope) mentors and counselors to their successors. The young generally have respect for their elders if those elders are, in fact, wise and nurturing, but this respect is meaningful to the elder only if there is *self-respect*. The key to self-respect is *significance*.

Significance

The fundamental question about anything we do in life is this: is it important enough to make it worthwhile getting out of bed in the morning? There's no objective measure of "significance." It's more an inner sense, different for each of us, and each of us will know quickly whether it's there or not.

It's not necessary for any of us to keep working like a lathered mule. What's important is to avoid the pasture unless (and until) we're sure we like munching grass all day.

I once met a business owner who was "retiring" at 55. The company he founded and built had been sold to his sons, and he was using some of the proceeds from that sale to start another business, one that would require only half of his time. With the other half, he planned to "see the world." We bumped into each other some years later in Dallas.

"How's the retirement?" I asked.

"It didn't work," he answered. "Remember that new business I started? It's now doing twice the dollar volume of the original business. I have to retire all over again."

It was significant, I think, that he reported this "failure" with one of the broadest smiles I'd ever seen.

The moral to that story is personal to each of us.

I'm sure you know what I mean.

9: Thoughts for Tomorrow's Owners

The silence is so thick, Jim thought, *you'd think the smoke alarm would go off.*

He looked across the kitchen table at his wife. Sheryl was staring down at her salad, playing with the lettuce in random, uncoordinated movements. The scrape of the fork skated across his nervous system.

The sudden fight had been totally unexpected. *Most of them are*, he realized.

He'd tried to tell Sheryl about some of the things happening at work. She wanted that. He tried to do it when he could. Now he remembered — again — why that usually wasn't a good idea.

"Uncle Sid mentioned bringing Sam into the company again today," he'd said to Sheryl, as he spooned dressing on his salad. "Dad asked what I thought, and I said okay. Sid really wants his son in, so we might as well get it over with."

"Did you remind Dad about your stock?" Sheryl asked, the tension almost immediately pulling at the edges of her mouth. He knew right away he was hurtling toward a long, long patch of black ice.

"Well…it didn't seem like the right time," he'd answered carefully, desperate to decelerate the conversation. "Dad doesn't want to upset Sid, and was tense enough about the whole thing without me adding another issue."

"Adding?" Sheryl shouted, her voice resembling the fork on her plate. "*Adding* another issue?"

"You don't understand…" he stammered, pumping the

brakes to control the horrifying skid.

"I understand perfectly, James Clark," she interrupted, and the black ice won. "Don't you ever again give me that pat on the head. I get more than enough of that from your father."

She set down her fork, slowly, with fierce calm.

"I understand the facts perfectly. You've worked for him and that greedy uncle of yours for 10 years, breaking your back and stretching our marriage to the breaking point, all for vague promises and out of some misguided sense of family duty."

He could only listen in sickened silence. The looming wreck was out of his hands.

"You're paid less than you deserve. You have no power, control, or influence. 'Someday, it'll all be yours' is an insulting joke they've told us too many times. You don't have the guts to stand up to them and demand the stock they promised, even though we agree again and again that you will.

"And, now, surprise, surprise, your cousin is tired of his life as a ski bum and wants to collect *his* half of what *you* built — and *you tell your Dad and Sid that it's okay because you don't want to* upset *them!*"

He'd seen a tear in the corner of her eye as she glared at him in silence. He almost longed for the blessing of hitting a bridge abutment head on, at high speed.

She was right, of course, but she didn't understand all the complexities, the politics, the loyalties, the frustrated dreams.

No surprise, there, Jim thought as the familiar depression pulled him down one more time.

I don't understand it, either.

Jim's not alone. In fact, he's a member of a relatively large minority group — but it's one that won't be found on any government lists.

There are no movies about the Jims of the world. They have no real organization, no national leaders. Generally, they don't even see themselves as a group. They are heirs and successors to business owners, a group usually seen by outsiders as members of a lucky sperm club, an overprivileged and under-endowed bunch of lucky ingrates who are "probably going to louse up the good deal that's being dropped in their laps."

Successors are isolated. Family insiders don't know how to

help. Outsiders see them as overprivileged. Ignored by the former and muttered about by the latter, successors don't understand their situation, either. Smart, capable, energetic, and talented though they might be, they end up hobbled and confused by this almost universal prejudice.

On one hand, they think they should be able to figure "it" out and do whatever "it" takes to get "it" done. On the other hand, in their isolation, they don't know where to begin or where to get the help they need.

CROWN PRINCE(SS) WITH AN IMAGE PROBLEM

If you are a member of this "lucky sperm club," it's essential that you recognize the importance of your role. Our economic future is in your hands. In spite of all the flip comments and prejudicial assumptions, you, as heirs and successors to today's business owners, are the ones who must preserve the backbone of our economy through the coming years. It is you who must build new and greater opportunity on the assets fate has entrusted to your care.

Other successors have done it in the past. You will, too. Your descendants are going to have to do it again.

You've got an image problem, however, in your own eyes as well as the world's. Succession to ownership just doesn't generate the excitement or the romance of *founding* a business. As most of us see it, it's the founder who braves bombardment and crossfire, disappointment and setback, discouragement and dejection, to build a dream. "The Kid," it's assumed, gets it all solely because he won the office gene pool, not because of any particular merit on his or her part.

That's the way most of the world thinks. Regrettably, that's even the way too many potential heirs and successors think, even those who don't have a career in the family's business. Notably, however, those who've successfully run the gauntlet of inheritance and transition, who own and manage the assets, generally have shed this sense of unwarranted privilege.

153

While it may be true they didn't get their jobs or wealth because of any particular merit, it's also true and more significant that they kept and built on both because they were tough, hard-working, and smart. They survived the crossfires, their own disappointments, conflicts and discouragements, to build their own dreams.

They have *earned* what so many others see only as an undeserved gift of Providence.

Those successful successors are now the owners. They've left the minority we're talking about here. Some remember what it was like, and manage to help the next generation onto a smoother, wider road.

Too many forget, however, and, instead, allow the whole difficult cycle to begin all over again.

A Mix of Blessings

If you are an heir to a closely held business, it is critical that you clearly understand the demands and requirements of that position, that you learn the full truth and operate on the basis of knowledge.

There are two sides to the business inheritance coin. The advantages just don't make up the whole picture, as most successors begin to suspect very early. Unless you understand completely what you're in for, you're going to end up with severely muscle-bound prejudices and problems of your own, as have so many others before you.

Along with the benefits of being to the manor born, you also inherit pressures, loneliness, frustrated expectations, and heavy, un-defined responsibility. In return for opportunity, you must accept these *and* the burden of having complex and potentially explosive assets placed in your hands.

This is the whole picture, one few successors are able to see and understand before they get deeply involved in either or both of the succession and inheritance processes.

The fact is, the benefits of inheritance are sometimes over-rated. The privileges of wealth often have some very sharp edges. Economic advantage is only a long-term benefit to those with the preparation, motivation, and talent to make something of it. Without such ability, the person with advantage can be in a short-lived and difficult position.

As a business heir, you *are* fortunate. No sense denying that. You have at your disposal many open doors, options that exist because you are the child of specific parents. Because of the position your parents hold in the community, you also have the acquaintance of powerful, successful people. You are more affluent than many, if not most, of your contemporaries.

But there are pressures, too, special challenges and demands that you share only with other heirs to closely held businesses. These pressures, more than the advantages, define the true uniqueness of your world. Fate is very evenhanded. It delivers every pat on the back with a mailed fist. With every privilege, a responsibility is delivered.

This is the other half of your inheritance, the half that's seldom recognized, let alone discussed, struggled with, understood, or acknowledged.

Working Heirs: Be careful what you wish for...

An heir who chooses to work in his or her family business is choosing a difficult and unique career path. It requires a combination of talents and abilities few people come by naturally. It requires management "techniques" that have yet to appear in established textbooks or the curricula of MBA programs.

Consider some of what will be required of you:

- You must prepare yourself for a job that's available to you independent of your preparation, or lack of it.

- You must gain the respect of everybody around you, when they "know" that you got the job solely because you're an owner's kid.

- You have to be objective about people with whom you've been emotionally involved since birth.

- You must, before you can have any realistic dream of your own, become deeply committed to and involved with somebody else's dream (i.e., the current owners').

- You must, on top of all that, become a competent professional manager with some key qualities of an entrepreneur, despite the evident fact that the two abilities are almost always mutually exclusive.

- Your job is to find a way to work into an existing (and relatively closed) organization. You have to be adaptable, tactful, smart, and flexible as an acrobat, while you successfully sell, administer, produce, and manage — all often in the face of a dubious and sometimes hostile audience.

The current owners, and their handpicked key people, are probably at the peak of their careers, careers that were built up with great pain and labor over many years. They have set the standard that you must now follow.

But you are new to the fight. You have yet to win all your hash marks and battle ribbons. For you, each accomplishment is a true victory, but to your elders and superiors, you're just learning. Didn't they do the same thing many years ago, when times (of course) were a lot tougher? Their early victories were breakthroughs. Yours, it seems, become little more than "about time." Repeating history just isn't enough.

Your predecessors built the train you're expected to board and ride. The founders laid the tracks. With every new generation, new cars, better engines, more freight and passengers were added. Hard work, all of it, and with each passing generation of ownership, the new owner-managers are asked to board an ever-accelerating train.

Building and growing is still the order of the day, but as a new heir, you have serious work to do long before you get to the creative stuff. You have to catch the train, which is moving very fast, indeed, and find a seat when seats aren't pre-assigned, and there's standing room only. If you complain this is a lot to ask, you will probably be called ungrateful. "Most people have to walk, you know."

The pinnacle of the current owning generation's success has now become your starting point!

I know of a business founded by an old-world craftsman and cabinet maker. He tried for years to make a living building cabinets, but couldn't compete with the cabinet factories. Through a combination of serendipity and shrewdness, he discovered the kitchen remodeling business, and his success grew.

The sale of his first remodeling job was a cause for celebration. He hadn't expected it. He was trying to sell his own cabinets when the customer asked him if he could install somebody else's. While he was at it, the customer asked, could he knock out a wall and redo a floor. Suddenly, he had a bigger job than he expected, but one which brought him more money with less work.

Today, 35 years later, his son and daughter work with him in his successful remodeling business. These two successors sell the same kind of jobs involving the pre-manufactured cabinets, relocated walls, tile floors, etc., but now, when they close a contract, it's not another success. There's no celebration. It's just business as usual, one more repetitive step in a frustrating and never-ending apprenticeship.

To make things worse, what they hear from the founder sounds like nothing but a string of deflating comments. He'll say, for example, that the only reason they sold the job in the first place is the good will *he's* built over the years. It's all in the company's name and reputation, he tells them. Besides, there's really no money in single cabinet-and-floor jobs any more. The big money's in selling the big developers on whole subdivisions of new kitchens. Then he tops all that encouragement off with the corker:

"In fact, this job may even wind up costing us money!"

Is all this unfair? Is some of it even untrue? Maybe, but the only real certainty is that it comes with the job.

It *is* unfair when teachers so easily and conveniently forget what it's like to be learning. It *is* unfair when successors are measured by standards that are artificially high or arbitrarily defined. It *is* unfair when successors are denied recognition of their legitimate victories solely because somebody else has done it before. It *is* unfair when anybody is judged on the basis of somebody else's history.

It *is* unfair, but it happens all the time.

Still, can we really say it's unfair to be asked to do more than those who came before us? The same challenge has been placed at the feet of every generation. To the extent that each generation learned to build on past efforts and knowledge, our civilization has progressed. Maybe we haven't advanced in skill and wisdom as quickly as we could have, but that doesn't imply that the challenges were unfair. They were only *difficult.*

There's a great difference.

Being Proactive about Your Career

The responsibilities that come with inheriting ownership in a family or closely held business are great, and much of this book is about how to define, understand, and manage those responsibilities.

When employment is added to ownership for an heir, however, the complexities grow enormously. Your very survival, spiritually, psychologically, and financially depends to a great extent on your ability to respond to and handle those complexities. Jim's discussion with his wife at the beginning of this chapter is evidence that he is not managing that complexity very well at all.

Jim and all of his counterparts can do better, but there are no simple answers, no panacea. Fortunately, the experiences of many others who have gone before you provide a few rules of thumb. These may help as you wend your way through that unique experience of being a "next-generation" owner-manager:

Start Elsewhere (when possible)

No matter how much you love the business, beginning your working career in a company owned by your relatives is almost guaranteed to be a mistake. The business may need you desperately. There can be a lot of pressure to "pitch in and do the right thing." Often, there can be no choice.

But where a choice is available, your own credibility, understanding, self-confidence, and knowledge are best built in the outside world. There you will rise or fall on your own merits, not the name above the door.

Also, outside experience has a direct, positive correlation with owner value. As the world grows more complex over the coming decades, more closely held businesses will be looking outside themselves for key managers with wider experience than the company has developed internally. Bring that experience, and you bring value.

It only makes sense to become qualified as one of those "outsiders" as early as possible.

Develop a Résumé

It is wise and prudent to build your career with an eye to employability — obvious, maybe, but a truth that's far too often overlooked. Whether or not you work in the family business, approach each job as part of a record on which you will be judged by prospective employers. The operative question should be something like, *"If I were to explain what I did in this job, would it be meaningful and impressive to a future employer?"*

Functioning as a general troubleshooter or a perennial student of internal management structure in the business is not enough. While interesting and educational, such jobs only tie tighter the apron strings of the family business. The skills you develop will be either unique to that specific business, or impossible to sell to others outside.

The lack of a résumé results in a lack of options, which leads to claustrophobia and insecurity. Under those conditions, you're even more likely to make bad decisions about your career path. The results can be disastrous.

Instead, focus on building a track record, something no one can take away from you. This is accomplished, specifically, through a devoted:

Focus on Performance

Accept only those jobs where you are certain performance will be defined and judged objectively. (See *Chapter 6* for a discussion of strategic compensation and performance measures.)

Insist on being held to clearly defined goals. Make sure you have the resources and skills to reach those goals. Make sure they are public and that your success or failure are public, also. This is the only way the current owners, your peers, advisors, suppliers, and customers will know if you are an asset to the business or not.

It's also the only way you will build essential credibility within yourself.

And, finally:

Work Like Hell

A FUTURE WORTH HAVING

The successful closely held business is a treasure vault of potential and opportunity being stored for future generations. It's something no "job" and few other investments can provide.

This is why failure to manage the value of a business is so wasteful, and why settling for a status quo of frustration, disagreement, misunderstanding, and conflict is unacceptable.

The worst thing about such failures is that nobody wants them to happen. They happen in spite of our wants and needs. They happen in spite of our hopes and expectations. They happen in spite, even, of our love for each other.

Built into the closely held business are almost all the tools necessary for success. The real lack is in the understanding, accommodation, and process necessary to put those tools to work.

As an heir to ownership and, potentially, management of your closely held business, you have the most to gain by success and the most to lose by failure. Much depends on your ability to recognize and learn hoe to use those tools.

You are being asked to accept a major responsibility. In many ways, all the stakeholders in the business, the suppliers, the customers, the employees, their families, your family, and your children depend on you to take a proactive, professional approach. If you fail in that responsibility, you not only let yourself down; you let all of them down, as well.

If you succeed, and it will take aggressive and proactive attention from you for that to happen, then one of the greatest economic ways of life available in our society becomes a viable option in the future of all the stakeholders.

You will, in fact, have played a central role in building the owner value of *your own* business.

Not bad for a life's work.

Cleveland, Ohio
June 29, 1996

APPENDICES

A-1: Buy/Sell Agreement Provisions

While much of the language in buy/sell agreements is standard wording, the core language in each agreement deals with specific questions unique to each company. What follows are sample paragraphs taken from actual agreements drawn up for multi-generation, multi-owner closely held businesses.

These are presented only as examples of how specific concerns could be addressed. *Qualified professional help in drawing up an agreement is essential.*

To begin, it's customary that the parties to the agreement and the stock distribution are listed, followed by a statement of objective such as:

> ...The parties hereto believe it to be in their best interests to restrict the transfer of such stock and any stock of the Company the Shareholders acquire in the future (the "Shares") and to provide for the orderly future disposition of the Shares if certain contingencies occur...

Agreements typically go on to state that

- All transfers of stock must meet the provisions of the agreement

- The company can be required to purchase offered shares subject to restrictions

- Certain gifts to lineal descendants of the founders can be pre-approved

- Voluntary transfers of stock are possible subject to restrictions such as stated below:

"...Shares shall first be offered for sale to the Company as provided...the Company shall have the option to purchase all (but not less than all) such Shares at the price and on the terms set forth below:

(a) If the Shareholder offers such Shares intending to sell or exchange such Shares, the Company may purchase such shares either (i) at the price and on the terms and conditions of the intended sale or exchange, as stated in the Shareholder's offer, or (ii) at the price and on the terms specified in [the sections on pricing formula and payment terms, see below] hereof, whichever the Company elects.

(b) If the Shareholder offers such Shares intending to transfer, pledge or otherwise encumber, or otherwise dispose of such Shares in any manner not described in [above paragraph], the Company may purchase such Shares at the price and on the terms specified in [pricing/payment sections].

In the event the company chooses not to exercise its first option to purchase the offered shares, non-offering shareholders are generally given second option. If non-offering shareholders don't want to purchase the shares, then they can be offered outside the company and shareholder group under the same terms as the original offer, subject to restrictions like the following:

...only (a) during a period of 30 days following the expiration of the shareholder's option, (b) solely to the persons or entities identified in the offer to the Company, and (c) only if such persons or entities, in writing, accept and become bound by all the terms and conditions of this agreement...

Involuntary transfers (levy, garnishment, attachment, divorce settlement) should also be covered, usually by both binding the new shareholder to the terms of the shareholder agreement, and by giving the Company first option, and other shareholders second option to purchase all shares transferred involuntarily. Terms for such an option could read as follows:

> ...(a) at the price and on the terms under which the Shares were acquired by such transferee or successor, or (b) at the price and on the terms specified in [pricing/payment sections], whichever the Company elects.

Death transfers must be dealt with also. Shareholders' survivors could be required to sell their shares to the company. Alternatively, a provision can be included to restrict transfers to lineal descendants only, as in:

> ...the surviving spouse may not gift Shares during life or at death to any subsequent spouse, the intent being that Shares gifted to or for the benefit of a surviving spouse be transferable only to lineal descendants of [founders, etc.].

Further restrictions can be placed on a surviving spouse's ability to vote the stock he or she holds:

> ...Shares held by or in trust for the surviving spouse shall be voted in equal shares by the deceased Shareholder's children who have attained age 21 or, if none, pro rata by the other shareholders...

An important provision usually included is one such as the following which is aimed at protecting the financial health of the company:

> ...Notwithstanding any other provisions of this Agreement, the Company shall neither exercise any option nor otherwise be obligated to purchase any Shares hereunder if the payments required to purchase the shares would render the Company unable to pay its debts in the ordinary course of business after any such payment.

Important sections of buy/sell agreements are those dealing with pricing formulas and payment terms. There are, of course, endless ways to define value. The final, agreed-upon formula is usually arrived at only after long and detailed negotiation among shareholders. Here's an example from an actual buy/sell agreement:

...Certificate Value per Share shall be determined by an appraisal performed by an independent appraiser selected by the Shareholders and the Company. For purposes of this Agreement, the Certificate Value per Share shall be an amount determined by dividing an amount equal to 85% of the fair market value of the Company by the number of shares of the Company then issued and outstanding. The Certificate Value per Share shall be revised biennially pursuant to an updated appraisal performed by the Appraiser as of the appropriate anniversary of the initial appraisal; provided, however, that on each sixth anniversary date a completely new appraisal shall be performed by the Appraiser or by a new independent appraiser, as agreed upon by the Shareholders and the Company.

Instructions to the appraiser regarding real estate are usually included, such as:

...the appraisers shall be required to use applicable standard appraisal techniques in conformity with guidelines and ethics of the American Institute of Real Estate Appraisers to form an opinion of the market value of the property(ies) owned by the Company...

These instructions can get very detailed. Some agreements today are even including provisions to exclude consideration in valuation of hazardous material exposure, or to define how such concerns should be handled (experts required, cost allocations, etc.). Here is an example paragraph:

...Unless specifically directed, the report should not take into consideration the possibility of the existence of asbestos, PCB transformers, or other toxic, hazardous, or contaminated substances and/or underground storage tanks containing hazardous materials. Further, the report should not consider the cost of encapsulation, treatment or removal of such materials. If there is a concern over the existence of such conditions in the subject property(ies), and if so directed, the appraiser must retain the services of a qualified engineer or contractor to determine the existence and extent of such hazardous conditions. Such consultation should include the estimated cost associated with any required treatment or removal of hazardous material which then must be incorporated into the determination of market value...

Provisions are often included defining "fair market value" of the ongoing business. An example:

> ...the discounted future distributable earnings method shall be used as the primary method of determining fair market value. In conjunction therewith, the appraiser shall analyze and normalize historical revenue and expense patterns and determine appropriate levels of net working capital and capital expenditures as functions of revenue. From the results of these analyses, combined with conclusions made about the projection, operational, economic, and regulatory environments as they may impact financial results, the appraisers shall determine pro forma debt-free distributable cash flows. Such cash flows shall then be discounted by an appropriate weighted average cost of capital and totaled to yield the present value for the invested capital. Interest bearing debt shall then be subtracted from the fair market value amount to yield the value of the shareholder's equity.
>
> ...in addition, no discount or reduction in fair market value shall be made as a result of any federal or state income taxes that might be attributable to the differential between the cost basis of the Company's assets and the fair market value of the Company's assets, irrespective of whether the Company is a regular C corporation or an S corporation for federal or state income tax purposes...

Sometimes consideration is given to devaluing minority interest, or, alternatively, all shares can be defined as having equal value as:

> ...No discount shall be applied to any Shareholder's shares as a result of a minority interest in the Company; nor shall any premium be applied to any shareholder's shares as a result of a controlling interest in the Company. It is the intent hereunder that all shares shall be considered to be of equal value.

Payment terms can be described in language like the following:

> ...the purchase price of any Shares purchased by the Company or any Shareholder pursuant to this agreement shall be

payable (i) in cash; (ii) at the option of such purchaser, in installments by delivery of a negotiable promissory not of the purchaser, payable in 48 equal monthly installments of principal and interest, commencing on the date of tender and bearing interest from the date of tender at the greater of ___% annually, or the mid-term applicable federal rate, monthly compounding, from time to time determined under Internal Revenue Code Section 1274(d), and providing that the purchaser may prepay any such note in full or in part at any time without penalty; or (iii) upon such other terms as the seller and purchaser(s) may agree. If the purchaser is the company, any promissory note shall be personally guaranteed in writing by the remaining Shareholder(s) on a joint and several basis...

Payment of insurance proceeds can also be covered:

...the Company shall pay to the legal representative of the deceased shareholder an amount of cash equal to the lesser of (i) the total purchase price of the deceased Shareholder's Shares, and (ii) one-half the dollar amount of any life insurance proceeds the Company receives from policies it owns on the deceased Shareholder's life, as the initial installment of the purchase price for such Shares. Any unpaid balance of said purchase price shall be payable in the manner determined in [above paragraph]...

Standard wording on closing, security for installment payments, and note holder protection is often included. Execution of the agreement requires endorsement of existing share certificates with something similar to the following:

NOTICE

The transfer or pledge of the Shares represented by this Certificate is restricted by, and subject to, the provisions of a certain Stock Buy and Sell Agreement between the Company and its Shareholders dated._____, providing restrictions on the transfer of this stock. A copy of said Stock Buy and Sell Agreement is on file at the registered office of the Company. By acceptance of this Certificate the holder thereof agrees to be bound by the terms of said Stock Buy and Sell Agreement.

Keep in mind that what I've presented here is only a sample of the kinds of provisions and powers that can be built into a shareholders agreement. *An actual document should always be drawn up with professional assistance.*

This introduction should be enough, however, to give you a sense of how useful such agreements can be. First, it will guide your planning process, since running the "disaster" and other transfer scenarios forces you to ask yourself and your advisors most of the important planning questions. Ultimately, it will help assure that your planning actually has the effect you intend.

A-2: Family Employment Policy

ANY COMPANY, INC.
FAMILY EMPLOYMENT POLICY

PURPOSE

Any Company believes that our success and growth depend upon employees who are as qualified and effective as possible. This is the highest standard we use in our hiring decisions. We encourage family members who meet this standard to consider and apply for employment with Any Company.

This policy is written to clarify the criteria and process for employment of individuals who are shareholders or are related by birth or marriage to shareholders of Any Company (from here on referred to as "family members").

Family membership carries privilege and responsibility which should be recognized by everyone. The *privilege* is that, assuming equal qualification and competence, family members will be given preference in hiring and promotion. The *responsibility* is that the company and the prospective family employee must, at all time, take great care to respect and abide by the stated standard that *only the most qualified and effective employees will fill positions in Any Company.*

This policy defines the process by which that standard will be applied in employment of family members.

PHILOSOPHY

Any Company is an integral part of its economic and social worlds. We take our responsibilities to our employees, their families, and community seriously. We expect all family members, whether employed by Any Company or not, to do everything in their power to become productive and contributing citizens. One principal responsibility comes from our success as a family in business: the duty to contribute to the community and the society that has given us so much.

We encourage all family members to concentrate on becoming — and helping others to become — moral and effective human beings. This requires *integrity*, the ability to integrate a sound ethical standard into all decisions and actions. This requires *maturity*, the ability to act appropriately in all situations. This requires *leadership*, the skill of directing and motivating others. This requires, perhaps most importantly, *followership*, the willingness to work well with others and to function as a productive team member.

Only those who demonstrate these traits will be employed by Any Company, whether they are family members or non-family.

We believe that these traits are best developed in environments that demand initiative, stretch abilities, develop self-confidence, and increase self-esteem. These experiences can take many forms, and they are not limited to employment situations. We encourage all family members to expose themselves to such experiences with openness and enthusiasm, because the resulting personal growth will prove invaluable in both work and family life.

In following this philosophy, we believe it best to think of employment of family members by Any Company not as a right, but instead as a privilege that must be earned. To that end, we have established the following guidelines for employment of family members.

FAMILY EMPLOYMENT GUIDELINES

1. Entry-level employment of family members by Any Company is discouraged.

2. Family members must meet the same hiring and performance criteria as apply to non-family employees.

3. Preference in hiring will be given to family applicants only in situations where family and non-family job applicants exhibit equivalent qualifications.

4. Compensation of family employees, whether it be in the form of regular pay or perquisites, will at all times be based on the following standard of fairness: that Any Company would compensate a non-family employee similarly for the same responsibility and performance.

5. A special Committee of the Board of Directors will be created and charged with the responsibility for monitoring all family employment situations and ensuring that they meet these guidelines.

NON-FAMILY EMPLOYEES

Nothing in this Policy should be taken to imply that non-family employees of Any Company are second-class citizens or less valued than family employees. In reality, Any Company will be able to succeed and grow only with the additional help of qualified and committed employees from outside the family.

The owners and family managers of Any Company dedicate themselves to building and maintaining a work and career environment where all employees, family and non-family, can find ongoing opportunities for growth and self-fulfillment. While we are interested in providing opportunity for family members to participate in building on the foundations laid by their predecessors, in no way will that desire be allowed to stand in the way of either the success of the company or the well-being of all its employees.

At Any Company, all members of the working team have both a significant part to play in our success and a right to benefit fairly from that success.

A-3: Sample Uncapped Incentive Bonus Systems

EXAMPLE I: AN EQUITY-BASED INCENTIVE

X COMPANY
Management Incentive System

Incentive bonuses will be uncapped and distributed from a profit-based pool. This means that the bonus pool varies with profit, with no upper limitation on absolute dollar amount *once minimum profitability targets are met.* Operational units must meet shareholder profit targets before bonuses can be earned.

ROI, for compensation purposes, is calculated on an "operating book value" basis. We have determined that book value is a fairly accurate measure of market value of X Company, so we used book value as a basis for compensation design, *adjusting the accounting number to reflect actual operating assets.* This is not a truly rigorous accounting procedure, but is considered by the Compensation Committee of the Board and by management to be a more appropriate way to measure the performance of management employees in operating the company.

In the figure immediately below (*Figure A-3-1*), "Company Net Worth" is the book value shown on the balance sheet, and includes

X Company Incentive Compensation Projections

Incentive Pool Share of Profits above Minimum ROI	15.00%	
Planned Sales Growth	15.00%	
Income Tax Factor	30.00%	
Minimum After-Tax Return on Investment for Incentive	10.00%	
Company Net Worth (Beginning Book Value)	7,850,000	8,585,420
Non-Operating Asset (NOA) Value for Adjusting Net Worth	1,255,000	1,286,375
Assumed Annual Increase in NOA Value	2.50%	

INCENTIVE COMPENSATION CALCULATION	1996 (Actual)	1997 (Plan)
Sales	45,550,000	52,382,500
Earnings Minimum before Incentive (Pre-Tax)	1,121,429	1,226,489
Actual/Plan Net Income before Tax/Bonus (NIBT)	1,050,600	2,873,704
Actual NIBT % of Sales	2.31%	5.49%
Earnings above Minimum	-70,829	1,647,215
Incentive Compensation Pool ($)	0	247,082
Incentive Compensation Pool % of Sales	0.00%	0.47%
Incentive Compensation Pool % of NIBT	0.00%	8.60%

ROI ANALYSIS (After-Tax Basis)	1996 (Actual)	1997 (Plan)
Sales	45,550,000	52,382,500
Net Income after Tax/Bonus (NIAT)	735,420	1,838,635
Beginning Net Worth (Assuming Total Reinvestment)	7,850,000	8,585,420
Operating Net Worth (Assuming Total Reinvestment)	6,595,000	7,299,045
NIAT % of Sales	1.61%	3.51%
Earnings Minimum as % of Net Worth (Minimum ROI)	14.29%	14.29%
NIAT % of Net Worth	9.37%	21.42%
NIAT % of Operating Net Worth	11.15%	25.19%

Figure A-3-1: Spreadsheet model used in calculating incentive pool amounts for illustration and planning purposes.

book value of land investments and other non-operating holdings which, while they have value to shareholders, are not *operating* assets. We have, therefore, adjusted accounting book value downward by the value of those non-operating assets to calculate the return on operating investments represented by operating earnings. ROI is properly calculated on an *after-tax* basis (and, of course, after incentive payments).

The last row in *Figure A-3-1* (NIAT % of Operating Net Worth) analyzes operating ROI of the year just completed, as well as that projected by the current management plan. Note that on this basis, *book* ROI in 1996 was 9.37%, while *operating* ROI was 11.15%. At these low levels, the after-tax net income was below the minimum required by about $71,000. Therefore, the incentive compensation pool was empty, thus, no incentive bonus was paid.

The Compensation Committee has reviewed the budget/plan presented by management with an eye toward achieving acceptable ROI in future years. We have determined that the absolute minimum return the shareholders can accept is 10% on book value. This has translated, roughly, into a minimum of 2.4% of sales, which becomes the profitability "floor" below which no incentive pool will be generated. Further, we have determined that ROI should be in the vicinity of 25%, which requires (see *Figure A-3-1*) NIBT levels at 5.5% and above, with sales growth rates of 15%.

The Bonus pool consists of profit in "excess" of a minimum shareholder target ROI. Note in the spreadsheet figure above, incentive compensation is based on two key standards:

- **Minimum ROI is 10%+ annually.** The "shareholder equity growth target" is what the shareholders define as an essential minimum return on their investment in X Company. This minimum in 1996 was $785,000 (10% of beginning book value) which was higher than actual after-tax profit, resulting in no 1996 bonus. Plan for 1997 is for $1.8 million profit after tax and bonus, which requires a pre-tax profit of $2.874 million.

- **Management Pool is 15% of Earnings above Minimum ROI.** Assuming 1997 targets are met, total above-minimum, after-tax earnings will be $1,647,215, 15% of which will be $247,082, or the 1997 bonus pool. Below (*Figure 2*) is an illustration of how compensation will look in 1997 if the company meets the plan.

Distributions from the pool are determined by supervising managers for subordinates at each level of management, limited to the amount of pool dollars available at that level. Share of the

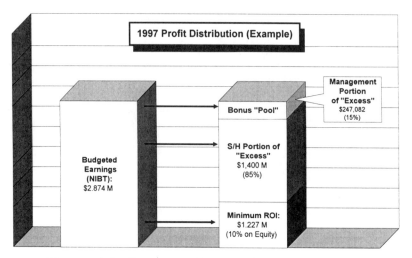

Figure A-3-2: *Illustration of bonus pool relation to minimum profitability and total budget earnings.*

pool at each management level will be determined by calculating a percentage based on dividing the *total base salaries at a specific level* by the *total base salaries for all managers in the system.*

Incentive goals will be determined during the budgeting process, and incentives awarded during formal annual reviews. As a defined responsibility, each supervising manager will be required to conduct formal reviews with each subordinate *annually.* These reviews are not optional, and written reports of each review will be signed by the reviewed manager and filed in that subordinate's personnel file. While total amount of a manager's potential individual share of the pool is defined on a relative percentage basis (his salary level relative to others), *actual bonus awards would be adjusted upward or downward based upon individual performance to individual goals.*

For example, if "manager x" had a potential bonus of $10,000, but he only achieved half of his personal performance goals, the actual bonus awarded during the annual review could be set by his supervisor at $5,000, and the reasons for the decrease discussed with him.

While no compensation plan is perfect, this plan has been

designed to meet three requirements:

1) The system must focus management on shareholder value and achieving defined returns.

2) The system should be driven by operational factors alone, with variables under the control of management.

3) The system should be as simple and easy to understand as possible.

Calculating "ideal" return on investment is always problematic, and fully a matter of shareholder judgment. There are some benchmarks, however, to provide a "minimum" ROI required to justify maintaining investment in a business. Consider the second-last row of *Figure A-3-1* Spreadsheet model used in calculating incentive

INDEX/INVESTMENT	AVERAGE CHANGE/RETURN (1925-1994)
STOCKS	10.19%
BONDS	4.83%
TREASURY BILLS	3.69%
CONSUMER PRICE INDEX	3.13%

Figure A-3-3: Typical returns experienced by investors over 70 years. The change in the CPI is included for comparison.

pool amounts for illustration and planning purposes., and compare those returns to economic statistics (*Figure A-3-3*) that show average annual total returns/changes over the past 70 years:

On a more recent basis, over the past 15 years, the S&P 500 stocks have returned 11.8%, which is not much different from the 70-year average. Note that *on the full book value basis*, X Company is projected to return **21.42%** on book value in 1997. The shareholders have determined that this return is acceptable and adequate. Note that the 1997 return for X Company shareholders *based on operating investment* (last row in *Figure A-3-1*), is projected at **25.19%**, a respectable return, given the added risk (over standard market risks) involved with ownership of our company.

EXAMPLE II: A PROFIT-BASED INCENTIVE

Y COMPANY
Base Salary and Incentive System

Bonus Compensation Plan Objectives

As the Compensation Committee explored various bonus compensation options, we were driven by three primary objectives:

1) Each operating division must provide a fair return to the stockholders of the Y Company before bonuses are paid to the employees.

2) The plan must be simple — simple to understand and simple to administer.

3) The plan must provide an incentive for each employee, which allows him or her to focus on company objectives in such a way as to increase shareholder value.

We believe the following compensation plan meets these objectives.

Plan Design

- Each of the two operating divisions will be charged by the Board of Directors with a unique target percentage return on assets objective, expressed as a dollar amount, which will represent the *minimum acceptable return* on the operating assets of that Division. The Chief Financial Officer will establish an accurate asset base for each Operating Division (based on the average assets for the previous fiscal year), which will be used by the Board to compute this threshold target amount, below which no incentive pool will be generated.

- Operating earnings for each Division will be arrived at by isolating the Holding Company expenses from the Operating Divisions, but attributing all other expenses

183

as directly as possible to the respective Divisions.

- The annual pre-tax Operating Earnings of each Division in excess of their respective threshold target amount will constitute a Pool, a percentage of which Pool will be distributed to the employees of the Division according to a distribution formula determined by the Compensation Committee, and approved by the Board, at the beginning of the compensation period.

- Within the Holding Company and within each Division the employees will be divided into three groups — manager level, salaried level, and hourly level. To qualify for participation in this plan, an employee must have a minimum of 12 months of employment. Inter-Divisional transfers during the period will come under the incentive distribution plan of the new Division.

- The Holding Company Pool will consist of the combined balance of both Divisions' Pools after distributions for each Division have been determined (see *Figure A-3-4* on *Page 187*).

- Outside sales people, because of the "bonus" nature of their commission structure, are not included in the plan.

There is no discretionary "individual performance" component used in determining individual bonuses in this plan, since financial results are the best determinant of performance. Hence, although employees and their supervisors will continue to discuss individual performance and ways to enhance it, profitability is a team result and employees will participate in incentives as a team. Performance will have an impact on merit increases for future periods.

Application of the Plan

Application of the Bonus Compensation Plan to each level is as follows (all percentages are set by the Compensation Committee at the beginning of the compensation period):

Manager Level

Initially, the Compensation Committee will review the salaries of each person at the Manager Level to determine if that person's current salary is appropriate for his or her job description and level of responsibility. This salary, after adjustments, if any, will become that person's Base Salary. The Base Salary will be adjusted thereafter only to reflect an increase in responsibility or to compensate for a change in the cost of living (i.e., an annual increase equal to the increase in the CPI).

Each individual manager will receive an annual bonus calculated as a percentage of the Pool. The percentage for each manager will be determined by the Compensation Committee, based on relative responsibility and potential contribution to profitability.

Salaried Level

Base. A salary range commensurate with the job description and level of responsibility, will be prepared by the Manager for each person within the Salaried Level, and must be approved by the Compensation Committee. Annual merit increases based on individual performance may take place within the salary range at the discretion of the managing supervisor. The salary range will be adjusted annually to offset changes in the CPI.

Bonus. A percentage of the Pool will be assigned to the Salaried Level by the Compensation Committee. This will then be distributed *pro rata* to each participant according to his annual salary following the close of the period.

Hourly Level

Base. Job classifications will be created at each Division for all hourly positions. An hourly wage range, commensurate with each job classification, will also be established. Annual merit increases based on individual performance may take place within the hourly wage range at the discretion of the managing supervisor. The hourly wage range will be adjusted annually to offset changes in the CPI.

Bonus. A percentage of the Pool will be assigned to the Hourly Level by the Compensation Committee. This will then be distributed *pro rata* to each participant according to his annual salary following the close of the period.

Maintenance of the Plan

- Each Division will conduct regular meetings throughout the fiscal year, to include all employees, for the purpose of reviewing operating results. In addition to examining results, however, these meetings will present the opportunity to educate employees as to what the numbers mean, as well as to analyze team performance and build enthusiasm for the future.

- Because of the sensitive nature of financial information such as this, the results presented at these meetings will be in projected on a screen rather than distributed in writing to each employee. Also, to foster interest and understanding of the plan by all employees, the year-to-date results, in percentages only, will be illustrated in an easily understandable fashion and posted for all employees to see.

- The Bonus for each Level will be calculated based on audited financial results for the fiscal year, and will be distributed no later than the last day of the month following the end of the fiscal year.

- As an adjunct to the Bonus Compensation Plan, each employee of the Y Company will participate in an individual performance review at least once per year. The written results of this review will be retained in the employee's personnel file. For employees at the salaried and hourly levels, this review will be used as the basis for awarding merit increases.

- Prior to the beginning of each fiscal year, the Board of Directors will review the Plan, including the distribution recommendations of the Compensation Committee, making adjustments as necessary, and will formally adopt the plan for the coming fiscal year.

Sample Bonus Compensation Calculation

The table below (*Figure A-3-4*) is an example bonus calculation. The numbers are fictional, intended solely for demonstration.

DIVISION A

Established Parameters
Operating Assets = $500,000
Minimum Acceptable ROA:
  13% or $65,000

Assumed Operating Earnings	$100,000
Less Minimum ROA	(65,000)
Bonus Pool Generated	35,000

Distribution
Manager Level
  Employee A @ 10% .... (3,500)
  Employee B @ 11% .... (3,850)
  Employee C @ 8% .... (2,800)
Salaried Level
  3% distribution/2 empl. .... (1,050)
Hourly Level
  11% distribution/30 empl. .... (3,500)
Remaining Pool: $20,300

DIVISION B

Established Parameters
Operating Assets = $400,000
Minimum Acceptable ROA:
  16% or $64,000

Assumed Operating Earnings	$85,000
Less Minimum ROA	(64,000)
Bonus Pool Generated	21,000

Distribution
Manager Level
  Employee A @ 7% .... (1,470)
  Employee B @ 6% .... (1,260)
Salaried Level
  11% distribution/8 empl. .... (2,310)
Hourly Level
  20% distribution/35 empl. .... (4,200)
Remaining Pool: $11,760

HOLDING COMPANY

Combined Remaining Pool $32,060
Distribution
Manager Level
  Employee A @ 8% .... (2,564)
  Employee B @ 6.5% .... (2,084)
Salaried Level
  4% distribution/3 empl. .... (1,417)
Hourly Level
  2% distribution/3 empl. .... (641)
To Retained Earnings $25,354

Figure A-3-4: Illustration of bonus pool determination and distribution.

187

A-4: Sample Capped Incentive Bonus System

The situation:

1) "Schultz" manages Division A, and has a base salary of $100,000. The "standard" bonus at his level in the organization is 20%. The following targets were set for Schultz, Division A and the company, as a whole:

   Company — 15% ROIC

   Division A — Budget.

   Schultz — Create and lead a "reengineering" team to greatly reduce cycle time in developing new products.

2) The company achieved a 16% increase in ROIC. Hence, the organizational multiplier was set by the Board of Directors at 1.1 (out of the 0.0 - 1.5 possible range).

3) Schultz's Division met budget and actually exceeded margin and profit targets. The reengineering team was established and achieved a remarkable 75% reduction in the time it took to bring a new product on line. His leadership was instrumental in this success. Accord-

ingly, the individual multiplier was set by his superior at 1.5 (out of the possible 0.5 - 1.5 range).

Schultz's $33,000 incentive bonus would then be calculated as follows:

$100,000 * .20 = $20,000 (Standard Bonus for Schultz)
$20,000 * 1.1 (organizational multiplier) = $22,000
$22,000 * 1.5 (individual multiplier) = **$33,000**.

Here is a table of example bonus ranges for "Schultz" under various multipliers:

Organizational Multiplier	Individual Multiplier	Calculation Formula	Bonus Amount	
0.5	0.0	$20,000 * .5 * .0	$0	*Minimum*
0.5	0.5	$20,000 * .5 * .5	$5,000	
0.8	1.0	$20,000 * .8 * 1.0	$16,000	
1.0	1.0	$20,000 * 1.0 * 1.0	$20,000	
1.2	1.2	$20,000 * 1.2 * 1.2	$28,800	
1.5	1.5	$20,000 * 1.5 * 1.5	$45,000	*Maximum*

Note that the application of this system is significantly discretionary, yet, by the nature of the multipliers, there are objective parameters available to make bonus determination both relatively straightforward and easily explainable/understandable.

A-5: Long-Term Compensation Options

These plans can be powerful strategic tools for building shareholder value, but the tax code has laid a lot of mines in the road. *Expert professional input is always required.*

STOCK OPTIONS

Stock options are used in cases where the owner(s) are faced with a need to compensate senior management in special circumstances where actual equity ownership is considered an essential feature. Examples of such situations:

- An "interregnum," non-family CEO who is asked to build a company in anticipation of eventual transition to family members

- A son- or daughter-in-law in a senior management position, whose spouse stands to inherit common stock in the family company, but is not employed by the company.

From the perspective of closely held or family companies, there are two basic ways to approach stock option plans: incentive stock options (ISO's) and non-qualified stock options. The principal differences between the two center around value determination and tax treatment.

Before looking at each, here are some design component considerations:

- *Redemption Agreement.* A written agreement usually defines the circumstances and process for repurchase of the distributed stock by the company.

- *Employee Protection.* The agreement generally states that repurchase is an obligation of the company whether the employee is terminated, retires, becomes disabled, or dies.

- *Termination Provision.* The agreement can force exercise of the option in the event of termination, and, in the case of ISO's, either allow holding of the stock for the capital gains qualification or require immediate repurchase.

Incentive Stock Options

ISO's are plans covered by special provisions in the Internal Revenue Code. The current (as of 1996) tax code relevant to ISO's allows a company to issue to an employee an option to purchase actual shares in the company at a predetermined fair market value (N.B.: which is defined by an *outside valuation*). This grant is not a taxable event, nor are any increases in company share value taxable to the employee while he holds the option. The employee has 10 years to exercise the option according to the Code (five years if a family member). If he exercises the option, tax consequences to the employee come about only when he sells the shares back to the company at a gain from his purchase price. His tax exposure is at capital gains rates if he has held the stock for at least two years after exercising his option, otherwise at ordinary income tax rates. This approach is more advantageous to the employee than to the company, assuming favorable capital gains rates, since the company cannot deduct the distribution (unless the stock is sold back to the company before qualifying for capital gains treatment).

Non-Qualified Stock Options

These plans function in a similar manner to ISO's, with the exception that value can be determined by the board of directors, and gains are treated as ordinary income to the employee when the option is exercised, resulting in an expense deduction to the company under current tax law. Hence, these plans can be more advantageous to the company.

APPRECIATION RIGHTS/PHANTOM STOCK

In situations where distribution of actual stock is not appropriate or desired, "phantom stock" (sometimes called "shadow stock") can be used to distribute pseudo-shares instead of a set percentage of growth. This gives the employee rights to appreciation that equals the change in value of an equivalent number of shares of company stock. The principal purpose of this approach is to avoid distributing ownership rights, and to prevent dilution of real stock ownership, while affording the employee the equivalent of growth participation. The employee's benefits are taxed as ordinary income only when the phantom shares are "redeemed" and deductible by the company when paid. (For further discussion of phantom stock programs and specific examples of contract provisions, see *Appendix A-6.*)

Example Plan Structures

"Benefit" to the employee is the cash value received when the phantom shares are liquidated. Tax treatment is not complicated, if you simply think of benefits under these programs as a form of accrued bonus.

Outright Grant

An employee can be granted (e.g., upon hiring or promotion to position of key responsibility) *appreciation rights* to a designated equivalent number of shares of company stock (the number of phantom shares granted depends on the objective of the program and the value per unit). In essence, this represents a contract by the company to pay the employee upon retirement, death, or termination, all or a percentage of the appreciation in value of the equivalent amount of stock which occurred during the period since the grant.

Example:

- A *written* contract:

- Grants 4% of increase in book value of X number of equivalent company shares

- Vested in 10% increments over 10 years

- Paid out in 10% increments over 10 years

Performance Bonus

Alternatively, phantom shares can be granted on an annual basis, either as a supplement to the incentive bonus or as an integral part of incentive compensation. Here, because the phantom shares are part of the bonus, they could carry both the basis *and* appreciated values. Under this kind of plan, the size of phantom stock grants can be tied to various levels of increase in shareholder value, as below.

Example: For different potential levels of ROI:

- 1 phantom share granted for a 4% ROI

- 2 shares granted for 6%

- … etc.

Depending on objectives, rights in a phantom stock plan can vest over time (five to 10 years), and pay out of value can be similarly extended to minimize cash drains on the company. Further, such a plan would appropriately require a non-compete agreement.

Valuation of Phantom Stock

The most difficult part of developing phantom stock/appreciation rights plans is determining how "value" will be defined. There is no legal requirement that outside valuation be used, and the associated expense makes this an undesirable option in most situations. Unfortunately, book value (unadjusted) is seldom a good measure of value appreciation or even of owner value of the business.

Not all valuation methods are appropriate for valuing phantom stock. In most cases, it makes sense to calculate current value, using current financial performance, rather than projections of future value, since our intent is to reward *actual* management performance, not *potential* performance. This is the reason, for example, that the common valuation method called "discounted future earnings" would not be chosen. Also, it is preferable to use a pre-defined (and simple) formula rather than attempting to define "market" value, which can be problematic.

Here are two approaches to valuing stock which I believe make the most sense for typical appreciation rights/phantom stock plans:

Adjusted Book Value

The "Shareholders' Equity/Net Worth" value on the company balance sheet can be adjusted to reflect certain realities that affect real value but can negatively affect book value. For example, long-term debt that is incurred to liquidate a retiring shareholder can be added to book value so the employee doesn't suffer from non-operational changes in the balance sheet. Similarly, non-salary distributions to shareholders that exceed a specified "fair" rate of return could be folded back into retained earnings. This is often the simplest and most straightforward approach to valuation, but it is not appropriate for all companies (e.g., those with little asset values but high cash flows).

Capitalized Earnings/Earnings Multiple

A business could be valued using a formula consisting of two variables: annual earnings and a required rate of return. Earnings can be actual earnings for a given year, a rolling average of, say, the past three to five years, or an "adjusted" earnings (see above), folding back certain distributions to shareholders. The concept is that an investor would expect a specific rate of return for an investment. Since we know the expected rate of return (we've defined it), and the earnings (from the financials), it's possible to "reverse calculate" the capital investment, or presumed value of the business, i.e.:

Earnings ÷ Rate of Return = Business Value
Example: $200,000 ÷ 20% = $1,000,000

"Earnings multiple" valuation simply uses the reciprocal of expected return as a multiplier, i.e.:

Earnings * Multiple = Business Value
Example: $200,000 * 5 = $1,000,000

Combination of Book Value and Earnings Based Methods

In circumstances where the owners of a business define value in both asset growth and earnings growth terms with about equal significance, the above two methods can be combined via averaging or weighting. (An example phantom stock valuation method is included in *Appendix A-6.*)

Special Provisions

Depending on circumstances and specific needs, phantom stock plans can be written with provisions such as these:

- *Accounting Procedure.* The specific method of accounting for an employee's phantom stock (e.g., individual bookkeeping account) can be defined.

- *Dividend Equivalents.* In companies that pay significant dividends, an employee's phantom stock account can be credited with equivalent per share amounts.

- *Extraordinary Events.* The Board of Directors can be given the authority to define "extraordinary and non-recurring" events that have material impact on book value or earnings (e.g., acquisitions, stock repurchase), which would then be eliminated from or added to book value or earnings for purposes of valuing phantom stock.

- *Vesting and Distribution Schedules.* Depending on "golden handcuff" intentions and cash flow concerns, credited phantom shares can vest and benefits be distributed over time (e.g., vesting: 20% annually over five years; pay out: 10% annually over 10 years).

- *Termination.* The plan can state that phantom shares expire in certain situations (e.g., termination with cause), and require that rights be exercised within a set period of certain events (e.g., within 90 days of termination without cause).

- *Controls.* Provisions can be added to set such things as a cap on the number of phantom shares issued, and/or a "sunset" date for the plan.

- *Compensation Committee Administration.* The authority to make relevant decisions and administer the plan can be given to a committee of the board.

NON-QUALIFIED DEFERRAL PLANS

Equity-based plans, like those described above, can be powerful tools for focusing key employee attention on long-term enhancement of owner value. However, in certain circumstances, such plans may be inappropriate, either because they are incompatible with given owner goals, or because they are not perceived as beneficial by the employee(s).

Take, for example, a company that has considerable land holdings that the shareholders prefer not to develop or use for their immediate highest and best use. Key employees would have a natural desire to build value in these holdings in order to benefit from a phantom stock program. This presents a conflict between shareholder and employee goals under the equity plans described above.

Even if a phantom program fits owner objectives, "old guard" employees, especially those who have been with the company for a relatively long time, may not be excited about an equity plan that promises benefit in the relatively distant future, especially when such benefits are based on expectations of performance from younger, untested managers.

There are also instances where growth participation plans aren't enough, such as in the case of the highly paid manager who finds that because of qualified pension plan regulations, his qualified pension benefits, as a percentage of income, decrease as his income increases.

There are tools available to handle such situations, where growth oriented plans aren't adequate for achieving long-term objectives. While not strictly "strategic" in focus, they can offer appropriate ways to reward long-term employees who have already contributed significantly to growth in shareholder value over the years. Further, they provide situation-specific tools that are often useful when designing long-term growth participation plans for management teams with great variance in age.

These unqualified plans break down generally into two major categories:

Supplemental Retirement Plans

These plans can be designed to restore benefits to employees who've been hurt by changes in the law regarding qualified plans. They also can be used to provide supplemental income in retirement. These fall under the category of Supplemental Executive Retirement Plans (SERPs, pronounced *"surps"*) and are usually designed by benefit specialists (who describe these programs using "buzz" phrases like "top hat" and "excess benefit"). They are very flexible plans involving few of the usual bureaucratic or fiduciary headaches. It is also possible for the company to recover its investment in such plans.

Income Deferral Plan

These are most appropriate for employees who don't require the full value of their current income and, instead, want to defer that income — and the concomitant income tax — to later years. Ordinarily such plans are simply a convenience offered by the employer for highly compensated employees, and there are no incentives or "golden handcuffs" involved. A "matching" program can add those motivational components by tying the match level to performance and rescinding the matching funds if the employee leaves before normal retirement.

A-6: Phantom Stock Program Provisions

There are many ways to design phantom stock programs. Since they are non-qualified plans, business owners are free to be creative and design a program that fits specific needs and employees. *Appendix A-5* puts these plans into the context of overall strategic compensation design. It should be read first. This appendix is focused more on the nuts and bolts of plan design.

Phantom stock programs usually take the form of a legal contract, which defines the plan, its provisions, and specifically how it works. The discussion below follows an outline similar to one you might find in an actual contract, and uses examples from real plans. These are only examples. *It is essential to review provisions and the final document with professional advisors.*

PURPOSE OF PLAN; EFFECTIVE DATE

It's always a good idea to tie compensation, in any form, to the goal:

> This plan is designed to provide incentives to encourage eligible employees to increase the shareholder value of X Co.

The effective date should be defined in the contract as a matter of form.

ELIGIBLE EMPLOYEES

Coverage/eligibility could be defined as follows:

"…those key employees of the company who are from time to time nominated by the president of the company and approved by the board of directors of the company."

NATURE OF INCENTIVE

The "phantom shares" would be defined as hypothetical shares of common stock awarded by the board under a written agreement stating terms and conditions of such an award. Often, for the purposes of calculation, each phantom share would be equivalent to a share of common stock, although closely held companies are likely to use other measures, such as capitalized, normalized cash flow. An award of phantom shares does not create either equity interest in the company or a claim on shares of common stock, and a statement to this effect can be included in the plan.

INCENTIVE GRANT

The accounting can be set up in the form of separate accounts maintained by the company in the name of each recipient, and separately maintained for each individual grant of a block of "shares" to that individual.

ACCOUNT EARNINGS

Earnings credited to the recipient can be in the form of dividend and/or appreciation in value.

Dividend Equivalents

If any dividends are paid on real shares, the agreement could state that the employee's account would be credited with an amount equivalent to dividends actually paid on each common share. Although, in an S-Corp., this provision would probably not be included.

Increase in Value of Phantom Shares

The plan could state that each phantom share will be valued on the date it is credited to the account and again on the date the agreement is executed for pay out (see valuation section below for approach). The difference between the two values will be the amount credited or charged against the employee's account. In effect, this is an appreciation rights plan, crediting the employee only with the increase in value of the shares involved. The underlying basis value of common shares at the date shares are initially credited to an employee's account does not accrue to the employee.

PHANTOM SHARE VALUATION

There are many ways to go about valuing common shares for the purposes of a plan like this. This is the greatest design challenge. (See *Appendix A-5* for a general discussion of phantom share valuation.)

Here is an approach one company used:

(a) The net book value is determined (as of either inception or execution date) in reference to the consolidated financial statements of the company at the end of the fiscal year preceding the relevant date.

(b) This book value is adjusted for "extraordinary and non-recurring" items, which, in this specific case were defined as follows:

> "....after elimination of the liquidation preference of any preferred shares, including any unpaid cumulative dividends, and after adding back the net after-tax costs to the Company of redemptions or repurchases of any of the capital stock of the Company, and any payments to any shareholder of the Company or any affiliate of any shareholder."

(c) This adjusted net book value is then divided by the total number of outstanding common shares, plus the number of phantom shares granted under the plan, to determine a per share net book value.

(d) Since book value is not a perfect measure of "share-holder value," this example company also capitalized earnings to obtain a value component. They used a 9.5 multiplier, or an expected rate of return of 10.5%.

The example company adjusted "consolidated net income" (profit after tax, charges and reserves), for "extraordinary and non-recurring" items as follows:

> "...after elimination of any preferred stock dividends for the period involved and after adding back the after-tax cost of any payments to any shareholder of the company, or any affiliate of any shareholder."

This "consolidated net income" is then divided by the average number of outstanding shares during the period, plus the number of phantom shares granted under the plan, to get a per-share consolidated net income.

This company also defined this figure for the inception date of the plan. This per-share consolidated net income was then multiplied by the earnings multiplier (theirs was 9.5 or a 10.5% expected return) to achieve an earnings-based per-share value.

(e) The book value and earnings-based values, per share, were then averaged to obtain a "fair value per share" of phantom shares.

(f) The plan can include a provision requiring the board of directors to make sure that extraordinary events don't skew the book or earnings values. Such adjustments protect the employee. This adjustment can also protect the owners (e.g., eliminating the effect of acquisitions or sudden windfalls of profit not related to operations). The example company had a provision that extraordinary book value increases (e.g., an acquisition) would be eliminated from calculation, but would be added into value in seven equal annual increases. Hence, if the shareholders made a $700,000 acquisition using their own capital, that increase in value would not be part of the phantom share value in the first year, although $100,000 would be added per year over the following seven years.

VALUATION DATE

This is the "execution" date of the plan, or the time the calculation of terminal value of the phantom shares is calculated. The date could be defined as the earlier of:

(a) Specific anniversary date (e.g., 10 years)

(b) The date of termination of employment (other than for cause, which would void the agreement), whether by death, retirement, or otherwise (e.g., sale or disability)

(c) The date on which all of the common shares or substantially all of the assets of the company are sold to a third party (including mergers and consolidations which place current shareholders in a minority position).

VESTING AND PAYMENT OF ACCOUNT

A vesting period can be defined (e.g., 5 years @ 20% vesting per annum), and a payout term set (e.g., 20%, plus accumulated interest, per annum over 5 years).

EFFECT OF DISTRIBUTION

Full payment of account balances would cancel phantom shares.

PLAN ADMINISTRATION

The plan can be administered by the board of directors, with a provision that it can be amended or modified at any time (for subsequent benefits only). Also, the plan could have a provision to adjust phantom shares to reflect any change in common shares outstanding (e.g., stock splits, stock dividends).

MISCELLANEOUS PROVISIONS

It's wise to note in the plan that there is no guarantee of employment inherent in the conferring of phantom shares. Also, employees who receive phantom shares should be placed appropriately in the priority of creditors (in essence, not collateralized, but ahead of the shareholders). Further, it probably should be stated that rights under the plan should be non-assignable and non-transferable. Finally, we should consider inclusion of some sort of non-compete clause as a condition for payment under the plan.

This is a fairly simple approach to equity compensation that can be administered with relative ease (the more complex the plan and valuation formula, of course, the more complex the administration). The principal purpose of this approach is to avoid distributing ownership rights, and to prevent dilution of real stock ownership, while affording the employee the equivalent of growth participation. Under current tax law, the employee's benefits are taxed as ordinary income and deductible by the company when paid.

A-7: Advisory Board Specifics

SAMPLE ADVISORY BOARD CHARTER

"The Advisory Board of ___ will serve as an informal body providing advice and assistance to shareholders, Board and management, as appropriate, on questions and issues related to management, corporate strategy, ownership transition and management succession. In this role, the ___ Advisory Board is expected to help the shareholders address ownership issues and establish a strategic vision, to help the Board of Directors manage the structure, compensation, and transition of senior management, and to help senior management reach a high level of performance driven actively by the overall goal of steadily increasing shareholder value.

"The shareholders and the Board of Directors expect that the Advisory Board will make recommendations on improving financial and management reporting systems, help evolve the details of the ownership transition plan, and develop a preliminary "draft" of the management succession plan. The Advisory Board will function in oversight and coordinating roles only, and will not replace or supplant ongoing relationships with existing corporate or personal advisors. Further, the Advisory Board will not be involved in ongoing operations."

EXAMPLE ADVISORY BOARD ESTABLISHMENT PROCEDURES

Advisory Boards should focus on a range of operational and strategic issues, from ownership distribution, structure and agreements, through setting targets and goals, to control systems, to financial reporting systems (e.g., operating and capital budgets) and management organization. Advisory Boards usually have the following specific objectives during their first year or so:

- *Meet formally at least four times during the year.* There could also be a number of committee meetings (e.g., Finance, Compensation) on an informal and ad hoc basis, but, for efficiency, these need not involve the full Advisory Board.

- *Establish a prioritized list of issues to be addressed and set a schedule for addressing them.* Early meetings of the Advisory Board would be devoted to orientation — review of the factual and financial information available — and an exploration of the key issues for the future. The Advisory Board would use these discussions to set its operating agenda as soon as possible. (See below for sample goals.)

- *Structure task forces and/or committees, as necessary, to explore agenda items and suggest appropriate solutions.* Detailed and exploratory work is usually more efficiently done in Board committees of three to four members. Formal meetings of the Advisory Board can then be devoted principally to discussion of Committee reports/suggestions and management of the overall agenda. Typically, advisory boards form compensation, audit (or finance), and strategic planning committees.

Compensation Committee Responsibilities

General Responsibility

This committee concentrates on three areas: management development for transition; analysis and refinement of the management compensation system; and establishment of a direction and timetable for management team development.

The Committee assists the Chief Executive Officer in designing a compensation system that encourages management and employee performance consistent with company goals and objectives. It also provides advice and review of the performance goals established by the CEO for the management team.

Typical Issues/Goals

- Develop a recommendation for restructuring and developing the management team in anticipation of strategic and key management changes (e.g., significant growth, retirement of current key employees)

- Analyze the current base, incentive, and equity compensation system and make recommendations for improvement to ensure management focus on increasing shareholder value

- Analyze current shareholder perks and benefits and establish an approach to managing these benefits in the future

- Establish a family employment policy and a process for encouraging employment opportunity for family members, if appropriate.

Finance Committee Responsibilities

General Responsibility

This Committee concentrates on issues relevant to shareholder value definition and management, capital structure, and financing. It also provides overview to the management of equity.

Specifically, this focus includes assuring appropriateness of shareholder agreements and estate plans, providing oversight of financing requirements, and developing management performance goals/measures derived from the established shareholder value targets.

Typical Issues/Goals

- Analyze operating and capital budgeting and reporting systems, and recommend improvements that will enhance decision making on the shareholder, board, and management levels

- Assist management with analyzing financing needs and with developing required financing relationships and instruments

- Analyze capitalization structure and individual shareholder estate plans, with particular attention to managing the impact of unexpected events (e.g., untimely death or disability of a shareholder), and maximizing both ease of stock transfer to the next-generation and income potential for current owners.

STRATEGIC PLANNING COMMITTEE RESPONSIBILITIES

General Responsibility

Of all the advisory board committees, this one has the responsibility that's both most important and most difficult to define. In general, this Committee is responsible to help the shareholders and key managers develop and maintain:

- A strong, appropriate, and adaptive culture

- Effective, creative, and credible management leadership

210

- Committed, flexible ownership.

The Strategic Planning Committee is charged with the broad responsibility of overseeing these components of success. In that capacity, this Committee is appropriately concerned, as situations dictate, with issues from management recruitment, through growth strategy and corporate vision, to assuring smooth management and ownership transition.

Typical Issues/Goals

- Analyze the existing shareholder communication "process" and make recommendations for improvement

- Develop a program for reaching agreement on an overall shareholder vision, with the objective of defining a "shareholder value" target that is meaningful to shareholders and useful in providing direction to management

- Articulate a corporate vision that translates into strategic and tactical objectives for the longer term success and growth of the business.

A-8: Advisory Board Agenda and Minutes

Any Company, Inc.
Advisory Board Meeting — January 30, 199_
(Holiday Inn — 9:30 a.m.)

Agenda

OLD BUSINESS

    A. Review of 199_ Operating/Capital Budgets

    B. Review of Sales and Market Situation

    C. Inventory Management Status Report

    D. 401K Implementation

NEW BUSINESS

    A. Discussion of Final List of Company Objectives

    B. Review of Effectiveness of Management Reorganization

    C. Discussion of Potential Advisory Board Expansion

Minutes

ANY CO., INC.
ADVISORY BOARD MEETING

October __, 199_

Attending the Advisory Board's twelfth meeting were:

Stu Smith

Steve Smith

Mary Rodgers

Ron Henson

Bill North

Don Jonovic

Discussion covered the following topics:

Old Business

Pension Plan Split. Steve Smith and *Bill North* reported that the need is to upgrade the present plan to comply with the regulation changes. This is in process and almost completed, with the result that many plan participants will experience a decrease in benefits. Further, the conclusion is that splitting the plans, while keeping the same plan administration advisors, is advisable.

Bill North and Steve Smith will continue to investigate a revised benefits formula, as well as the possibility of dropping the plan in favor of a 401K plan. Decision will be made by December 31.

Medical Insurance. There was some discussion about the large increase from X, the current carrier, requiring consideration of a switch to Y, a new carrier.

Bill North and Mary Rodgers will explore options and rates, and intend to have the transfer accomplished early in November.

Sand and Gravel Operation Capital Budget. Mary Rodgers reported that the capital budget for the Toledo operation has yet to be developed. She said that with the switch to a new accountant, development of a capital budget will become a priority item.

Mary Rodgers will ensure that Ginny Malloy will work closely with Bill North to develop a Sand and Gravel Operation capital budget.

Ron Henson Compensation. Mary Rodgers said that the definition of *Ron's* compensation was complete, but had not been reduced to writing. *Ron* agreed. Given that it has taken longer for Ron's efforts to result in sales, a significant portion of his compensation in 199_ will be in the form of bonus, with the commission plan to commence in 199_. Further, the original sales quotas have been changed to reflect recent experience.

Performance Trend Data. Don Jonovic requested that *Bill North* include more trend data in the monthly financial reports. *Bill North* agreed to develop trend reports on selected information as soon as possible, but cautioned that data prior to 199_ would probably not be available.

Bill North will provide more trend data in financial reports.

Cost of Materials. Bill North and *Mary Rodgers* were not fully in agreement about the level of communication occurring between *Ginny Malloy* and *Bill. Mary* reported that *Ginny* was exploring the possibility of separating operating costs from capital costs for P&L purposes. She said they had costed out 90% of the Sand and Gravel Operation's business to capture what's actually capital investment. *Bill North* agreed this was a good idea, but that he remained concerned about the use of cash. Negative cash flow, he pointed out, could easily be much higher than any income statement loss.

Banking Relationships of Sand and Gravel Operation. Bill North said he would take part in the bank negotiations in November. *Mary Rodgers* said that the bank was asking for personal guarantees, which she was willing to give. *Don Jonovic* urged Mary to make sure that personal guarantees were spread out to minority, non-family owners (i.e., *Ron Henson*).

Bill North will help the Sand and Gravel Operation in bank negotiations. **Mary Rodgers** will look at broadening the "reach" of personal guarantees.

Financial Performance. Bill North reported that the revenue shortfall (and hence the drop in bottom line from budget) was mainly due to high fuel prices. *Steve Smith* explained that the depressed Sand and Gravel Operation revenue could at least partially be attributed to inadequate marketing efforts. The addition of *Joe Abrams* should help this greatly. *Bill North* noted the 21% return on investment, which he said was a very positive result.

Steve Smith will develop profitability tracking reports specifically to track **Joe Abrams'** performance.

New Business
Ron Henson Performance. Don Jonovic asked how *Ron's* association

with The Sand and Gravel Operation was working out. *Mary Rodgers* replied his impact has been positive. She believes the continuing positive climate is principally due to *Ron's* attention.

Next Board Meeting
The date of the next Advisory Board meeting was set for January 30, 199_.

A-9: How Formal Outside Boards Can Fail

As a source of outside review and advice, the formal, outside board is a vast improvement over the typical, inside board found in most family corporations. However, in practice, even outside directors can run into severe and sometimes insurmountable roadblocks which deflect them from their course and prevent completion of their mission.

Two key differences between outside boards in public companies (regulated boards) and those in closely held companies (private boards) provide the foundation for these barriers:

- *Lack of Authority.* Outside directors on private boards do not, generally, operate with binding authority. While it is true that such directors have voting power in board decision making, the relative smallness of the shareholder group gives a sobering reality to shareholder "veto" power over board decisions.

- *Lack of Definable Shareholder "Interest."* The shareholders of a closely held company, by definition relatively few in number, are not a group whose interests can be statistically distributed along a normal curve. Thus, for an outside director on a private board, acting

in the shareholders' "interest" becomes a near impossi-
bility, except in the most superficial and general of
senses. As any experienced consultant, advisor or family business member knows, there are usually a number
of powerful individual interests in a closely held company, and those interests are more likely than not to
diverge widely.

Thus, the outside (and, for that matter, inside) director on a
private board is likely to find himself or herself in a position where the
legal definition of the director's job — acting as overseer in the
shareholders' interest — is correlated with neither the clarity of the
responsibility nor the authority available for carrying it out.

Despite those limitations, however, properly managed and
implemented, a private board of outside directors can turn its attention
from the traditional shareholder-protective functions of a public
company's outside board toward a more general and advisory, (and
much needed) outside review capacity. This metamorphosis is, in
practice, difficult to achieve, however, because of the almost inevitable operational "aura" pervading meetings of a board.

INAPPROPRIATE "PROTECTION"

The public-company board serves as a protector of shareholder
interests. Private boards in closely held companies, quite naturally,
take on this traditional role, almost unconsciously, and often, I
believe, inappropriately.

I recall a meeting of an outside board during which the outside
directors took on the role of advising the successor/chief operating
officer on the "realities" of business. The successor/chief operating
officer was young and somewhat naive, and his stubborn confidence
in his own opinions was a major frustration for his father, the founder.
The directors took their cue from the founder and stepped into their
"protector" role.

The inappropriateness of this struck me in the closing part of the meeting when the successor suggested an untested marketing idea that would require an investment of $20,000. It was a creative, but risky idea, the sort of action entrepreneurs often implement without much analysis (essentially market research through marketing an actual product). The board, noting that the project had not been justified with detailed financial analysis, requested that the young operating officer "run the numbers" first, and report at the next meeting.

This advice was prudent, clearly, but also had the effect of dampening the successor's enthusiasm for the project. The board delayed his implementation of the project for at least six months, and set a very cautious tone — all to protect the successor and the shareholders from a minimum-risk, $20,000 investment in a very profitable, $7 million business. Taking a "protector" role in an essentially entrepreneurial business, this board mistook the real area of help needed — allowing the successor to take public risks and learn from the resulting success or failure.

Perhaps a group of advisors, created with an eye toward helping the internal management develop tools and techniques for managing risk, might have been better able to respond to this situation, which was, after all, more about management development than it was about protecting the shareholders' interests.

MISPLACED "DIPLOMACY"

Men and women typically chosen as outside directors are people very sensitive to power and its use. They are, consequently, sharply attuned to sources of influence and, yes, disruption among shareholders, family managers, and inside directors. Fully cognizant of his or her own fundamental lack of authority, the outside director can be placed under powerful pressure to join the emotional and political maneuverings existing in the private company boardroom as the only way to get things done.

If the business owner is stubborn, or sensitive to criticism, for example, the outsider is powerfully tempted to go a little easy. If the successor is not performing well, but the owner is blind to it out of love or hope, the outsider can become convinced that it is prudent to "give it a little more time."

In one family company in a northwestern state, two major divisions were run independently by a son of the founder and a son-in-law. While both successors worked together well enough for some time, the organization had evolved this way more for family reasons than for business reasons. The founder was attempting to be fair and equal in his treatment of his son and his daughter (through the son-in-law), and this division seemed to give each branch of the family their own piece of the business.

A few years ago, this company created an outside board, both to assist with strategic direction and to help mediate growing disagreements between the son and son-in-law. It became evident quite quickly that, although the two successors were talented and committed, neither was obviously chief executive material. Moreover, this company had poor financial reporting, and authority was fragmented haphazardly among the founder and the two successors.

The outsiders on the board realized that, along with reorganization, the company needed a controller and a chief executive officer, both of whom would have to come from outside the family and the company. But, because the founder's main agenda (over which he agonized in discussion with the outside directors) was treating his successors fairly, the outsiders did not push for reorganization at the outset. They concentrated, instead, on questions of shareholder value, return-related performance measures, and incentive compensation — operational issues that desperately needed attention, but with which the directors had little experience.

Eventually, a major reorganization was accomplished and a chief executive and a professional controller were installed, but this action was not precipitated by outside review so much as by two years of major operating losses and failure of a critical project.

In the end, this board did its job, perhaps in the only way it was realistically possible. But we could wonder what more timely effect *professional advisors* — a group led by professional practice and qualified by experience to question the financial and structural assumptions underlying this poorly structured organization — might have had on the situation.

PRESUMED "SYNERGY"

Most gatherings of men and women good and true tend to wrap themselves in cloaks of collective wisdom. When such a group is defined as a board of directors, it tends to secure that cloak with a golden clasp of infallibility.

A case in point is a manufacturing/distribution company that was having significant operational problems. This company had an "ideal" outside board composed of the owner and five outside directors. The board, recognizing the weaknesses of the owner in the area of financial management, prevailed upon him to promote the controller to chief operating officer.

The new COO was intelligent, confident, articulate and earned the full confidence of the board in his new role. Over time, however, the owner began to have grave doubts about his COO's true performance. The board, impressed with this young leader, prevailed upon the owner to ignore his doubts and continue him in his position to strengthen the financial performance of the company. (This kind of guidance, after all, was one of the owner's primary reasons for creating the board in the first place).

Without a doubt, the young COO did a superb job in some areas. Board meetings proceeded professionally, and the COO, a former auditor for a major accounting firm, presented operating results skillfully. The directors judged they had made the right decision in his appointment which led them to accept and follow his leadership as sound and his recommendations as valid. His ability to "sell" the board opinions as facts and interpretations as reality, lulled them into ignoring some major areas of evolving weaknesses in the company which, in fact, was headed into severe trouble.

This board fulfilled every definition of the classic outside board. The directors were successful business owners, independent, "risk-taking peers" of the owner. Their understanding of management and organization was more than adequate. Their grasp of financial analysis, however, was weaker than the Chief Operating Officer's. One cannot help but consider that a different definition of "outsider(s)," possibly one that allowed for an independent professional auditor, might have saved this company, its owner, and even the COO (who was eventually asked to leave) a great deal of grief and money.

The significance of this story is not that it's true, but that it's not unusual. It demonstrates the reality that the very nature of the closely held company often flatly precludes constructive creation and use of a formal, outside board. To be of real use, a board requires clear definition and proper management. But managing a board of directors is a complex task, requiring attention, preparation, careful planning, and time. These are, generally, the commodities in shortest supply in the family business.

The result? Most outside boards in closely held companies become more a hindrance than a help because they are formed before the necessary evolution, preparation and development occurs in the business. While that development process is occurring and, in fact, to help move the process along, the necessary outside review is better provided through an advisory board comprised, principally, of the owner(s) and key advisors to the business. (See *Chapter 4* and *Appendices A-7* and *A-8.)*

A-10: Board of Directors Policy

The shareholders of Any Company realize that the long-term success of the organization depends upon assuring a continual review of the policies, goals, and performance of the Company and its management. Further, the shareholders of Any Company believe that effective review of corporate and management performance requires a balance of inside and outside viewpoints. To this end, the Shareholders have decided to open membership of the Board to outside directors, and to formalize the functions and responsibilities of its Board to achieve this balance. This document has been created to assure that all shareholders, directors, and managers understand the Board's purpose, function, responsibilities, and charter.

BOARD PURPOSE

In general, the composition of the Board of Directors must be appropriate to the strategic and operational needs of the Company. Directors must periodically reassess the direction of all parts of the business to ensure that plans are in place to maintain and enhance the health and vitality of each part of the operation. To that end, the shareholders expect the Board of Directors to reassess, periodically, the direction and performance of the entire business, to examine and explore new avenues of opportunity, and to decide which current businesses should be redirected or disposed of. These are difficult and sensitive issues, and they deserve the clearest thinking and most creative approaches possible. Consequently, the Board must be comprised of people who are capable of making a truly meaningful contribution to this process.

DIRECTOR RESPONSIBILITIES

The directors of Any Company have a fiduciary duty to protect the interests of the shareholders. This translates into a dual responsibility to protect the shareholders' interest(s) and to help assure the long-term success of the corporation.

Specifically, these responsibilities translate into the following duties:

- To formulate company policy,

- To develop and set long-range objectives, and

- To oversee the implementation of the strategic plan and long-range vision of the company.

In this capacity, the Board of Any Company is expected to maintain an understanding of the goals and objective of the shareholders and to help the chief executive officer of the Holding Company lead management toward the achievement of those goals and objectives. As a matter of policy and custom, the Board of Directors of Any Company is expected to assiduously avoid involvement in the day-to-day affairs of the business, which are considered to be the sole domain of management.

Directors of Any Company, inside or outside, are expected to be loyal to the corporation. Directors are expected not to use their positions for personal gain or benefit without full disclosure and approval of the Board. Further, directors of Any Company will be privy to confidential information as a necessary requirement for carrying out Board responsibilities. Directors of Any Company may not disclose such information to outsiders or any person or organization without specific approval of the Board.

Directors of Any Company are also expected to pay the required attention to matters of importance to the corporation. Directors are expected to attend all Board and appropriate committee meetings, and to carefully review all information provided by management or the shareholders prior to those meetings.

Directors of Any Company, most specifically, are responsible for directing corporate management. In practice, this involves reviewing and approving management recommendations on major issues. Such issues include corporate policies, amending bylaws, declaring dividends, overseeing pension plans, determining executive compensation, approving long-term debt arrangements, reviewing long-range plans, approving capital expenditures and sale of assets, and advising shareholders on proposed acquisitions or mergers.

CHAIRMAN OF THE BOARD

The Chairman of the Board of Any Company is responsible for developing meeting agendas and for assuring that all directors receive appropriate information at least one week prior to meetings. The Chairman is also responsible for assuring that accurate and timely minutes are distributed to all directors as soon as practicable after each meeting.

The Chairman may, at the discretion of the Board, be an inside or outside director. He or she is expected to function as meeting parliamentarian, but, more importantly, is expected to guide and discipline discussion to focus on agenda items in a positive and constructive manner, encouraging and managing discussion, as appropriate to meet those ends.

Given the fact that management will always have a greater understanding of day-to-day operations than the non-managing directors of the company, it is relatively easy for the CEO/President to dominate Board discussions, consciously or unconsciously. A significant responsibility of the Chairman is to provide a conscious balance to this valuable expertise of operating management, to ensure that the Board discussions are characterized by a balance of inside versus outside viewpoints.

COMMITTEES OF THE BOARD

Committees of the Any Company Board of Directors are established to assist the full Board in carrying out its responsibilities and managing its ongoing work. In that capacity, Committees do not have any formal power. They serve principally to advise the full Board on matters important to its deliberations. Membership on committees can consist of directors and certain non-directors (e.g., Chief Financial Officer, who may not be a director), as appropriate.

Established committees of the Board are: Finance, Compensation, Nominating, and Strategic Planning. Functions and charters of these committees are as follows:

Finance Committee

This Committee, which will also carry out the traditional functions of an "audit committee," is charged with the responsibility of advising the Board of Directors on all matters related to capital, funding, accounting, budgeting, and investment for the corporation. Specifically, the Finance Committee will be responsible for:

1. Developing and recommending appropriate legal and capital structures for all operating entities.

2. Formulating dividend policy and annual dividend levels for all operating entities.

3. Reviewing with the Chief Financial Officer and the company's public accounting firm selected accounting and reporting procedures, and advising the Board as appropriate.

4. Reviewing and assessing financial control systems, and advising the Board as to required adjustments and/or changes.

5. Reviewing and making recommendations to the Board as to the sources and uses of cash.

6. Advising the CEO and Chief Financial Officer on any matter pertaining to financial and accounting questions that may arise.

Representation: This Committee will consist of the Chief Executive Officer, the Chief Financial Officer, at least one share-holder/director, and an outside director experienced in financial matters.

Compensation Committee

This Committee is charged with the responsibility of assuring that the overall compensation programs of Any Company are effective and appropriate to the company's culture, mission, and strategic objectives. To this end, the Compensation Committee will be responsible for:

1. Reviewing the performance of the Chief Executive Officer and determining his or her compensation.

2. Assisting the Chief Executive Officer in designing a compensation system that encourages management and employee performance consistent with the goals and objectives of Any Company.

3. Reviewing performance goals established by the Chief Executive Officer for the management team.

Representation: In order to assure objectivity, this Committee will consist of outside directors only.

Nominating Committee

While the rotation of directors on the Any Company Board of

Directors is controlled by the election process, the shareholders of the Company believe their interests and the interests of the Company are best served through a careful rotation of directors over time. To this end, the shareholders expect that periodically the names of people with exceptional foresight and ability will be brought to the attention of the Nominating Committee by individual shareholders and directors, with the expectation that they could make a significant contribution to the organization.

The Nominating Committee of the Board is charged with the responsibility for maintaining a list of candidates, assessing the potential contribution of suggested candidates, and making recommendations, as required, to the shareholders of additional or replacement directors.

Representation: This committee will consist of a balance of inside and outside directors.

Strategic Planning Committee

This Committee has both the most important responsibility of all Board committees and the most difficult responsibility to define. The Shareholders of Any Company believe that the Company will continue to succeed only to the extent that the Company is able to maintain:

1. A strong, appropriate, and adaptive culture;

2. Effective, creative and credible management leadership;

3. Committed, flexible ownership.

The Strategic Planning Committee is charged with the broad responsibility of overseeing these components of success, and making whatever recommendations necessary to develop and maintain them. In that capacity, this Committee is appropriately concerned with issues from management recruitment, through strategy and vision, to management and ownership transition.

Representation. Membership of this Committee will consist of a balance of inside and outside directors, and its deliberations will, as appropriate, include professional advisors and members of the management team.

DIRECTOR TERMS

Directors of Any Company serve on an annual basis and are elected by the shareholders at their annual meeting.

MEETING FREQUENCY

Formal meetings of the Any Company Board of Directors will be held quarterly, and will be scheduled 12 months in advance. Special meetings may be called from time to time at the discretion of the Chairman. Meetings of Board Committees will be called as needed by the Chairman of the Committee.

DIRECTOR FEES/EXPENSES

Outside directors of Any Company receive a director fee, payable quarterly, the amount of which is determined annually by the shareholders. Meetings (regular, extraordinary, and Committee) are compensated on a per diem, determined annually by the shareholders. All normal and appropriate expenses incurred by directors in performing their duties are reimbursed by Any Company.

A-11: Retirement Planning Model

The following model can be a guide for building a spreadsheet for use in ownership transition and strategic planning. It takes into account the key variables inherent in financing owner retirement and business growth concurrently. Principally, these variables are:

- Projected operating results (cash flow generation)

- Net costs of retiring/liquidating owners

- Net costs of growth plans (capital investment, acquisitions, etc.)

- Net available cash flow after above retirement and investment costs.

Each organization and ownership situation is unique, so the model you ultimately use will vary from this basic structure. Whatever the final form your model takes, however, the exercise of designing it can be very eye-opening, sometimes sobering, and almost always of great interest to your principal lenders.

STEP 1: BASE CASH FLOW CALCULATION

For an appropriate number of years into the future, estimate the cash flow that can be expected from ongoing operations, independent of any significant investment for growth or payouts to retiring shareholders:

	Year 1	Year 2	...	Year n
Cash from operations				
Net income				
Add depreciation				
Add amortization				
Add/Subtract other				
Subtotal (a)				
Cash used for *existing* investments				
Acquisition/investment pay out				
Other				
Subtotal (b)				
Cash gained/used in financing				
Cash from borrowings[1]				
Less debt repayment				
Other (inputs/outflows)				
Subtotal (c)				
EXPECTED CASH FLOW I[2] (Sum of Subtotals a, b, and c)				

[1]Some borrowing may be required to maintain positive cash flow.

[2]From operations, before impact of retirement or future growth acquisitions and/or investments.

STEP 2: RETIREMENT CASH EFFECT CALCULATION

Calculate the effects of retirement of owner-managers on cash flow. Remember to consider both the positive impact on cash flow of lower outlays for salary as well as the negative effect on cash flow of reduced salary expense deductions:

	Year 1	Year 2	...	Year n
EXPECTED CASH FLOW I[1] (a)				
Cash effects of retirement program				
Add salary and fringes				
Less tax effect (decrease in deductible expenses)				
Less retirement costs/payouts				
Plus tax effect (greater expenses)				
Net retirement cash effects (b)				
UNALLOCATED CASH FLOW I[2] (Sum of a and b)				

[1]From operations, before impact of retirement or future growth acquisitions and/or investments (from Step 1).

[2]After retirement program, assuming no acquisitions or growth investments.

235

Step 3: Investment Cash Effect Calculation

The most "creative" part of the analysis, this growth investment plan should calculate the cash effects of a growth program. These could be either acquisitions or significant capital investments. A similar analysis can be done for both, and they can be combined:

	Year 1	Year 2	...	Year n
EXPECTED CASH FLOW I[1] (a)				
Direct acquisition cash effects				
Acquisition A (x% financed)				
Acquisition B (y% financed)				
Acquisition C (z% financed)				
Subtotal: direct cash effects (x)				
Cash effects of financing				
Add new borrowings cash impact				
Less cash out for new debt service				
Subtotal: financing effects (y)				
Cash earnings from acquisitions				
Add earnings required (hurdle rate)				
Less expected tax on earnings				
Add tax benefits (e.g., depreciation)				
Subtotal: earnings effects (z)				
NET CASH EFFECTS OF INVESTMENT (b) (Sum x, y, and z)				
UNALLOCATED CASH FLOW II[2] (Sum of a and b)				

[1]From operations, before impact of retirement or future growth acquisitions and/or investments (from Step 1).

[2]After future growth/acquisition program, no retirement costs.

STEP 4: NET CASH EFFECT CALCULATION

This final step in the analysis calculates the combined effects on cash flow of the retirement costs and the growth program:

	Year 1	Year 2	...	Year n
EXPECTED CASH FLOW I[1]				
Net retirement costs[2]				
Net cash effect of investments[3]				
Subtotal				
NET UNALLOCATED CASH FLOW[4]				

[1]From operations, before impact of retirement or future growth acquisitions and/or investments (from Step 1).

[2]From Step 2.

[3]From Step 3.

[4]Net cash flow per year, assuming both programs in place.

Index

The Ultimate Legacy

Receive the right advice from the Family Enterprise Institute.™

The Family Enterprise Institute™ was established to help owners of closely-held and family businesses like you find the resources they need to achieve their goals for the continuity, profitability and growth in value of their businesses. We can mail you free information directed specifically toward your needs, helping you to build *the ultimate legacy*.

On the attached member service card, request free literature by circling the numbers of individual issues covered in Dr. Jonovic's book, **The Ultimate Legacy: How Owners of Family Owned and Closely Held Businesses Can Achieve Their Real Purpose.**

Free information for owners of family businesses—fill out and mail the postage-paid card below.

Family Enterprise Institute™   **READER SERVICE CARD**

Name _____

Title _____

Company _____

Type of business _____

Street _____

City _____ State _____ Zip code _____

Telephone _____

SURVEY QUESTIONS

1. How much income did your company produce last year? ($MM)
   a. under 0.2   b. 0.2 - 0.4   c. 0.5-0.9   d. 1.0 - 9.9
   e. 10.0 - 99.9   f. 100.0 - 999.9   g. unknown

2. What was your income level last year? ($K)
   a. 0-75   b. 76-100   c. 101-150   d. 151-500   e. 501-750
   f. 751+   g. unknown

3. How many people work at your company?
   a. 1-25   b. 26-50   c. 51-100   d. 101-200   e. 201-250   f. 251+

4. Are you an original owner or a first, second or third generation owner?
   a. original   b. first   c. second   d. third   e. other

5. How many times in past year have you used an outside source of advice:
   a. 0   b. 1-5   c. 6-10   d. 11-20   e. 21+

Please rush me free information about the following topics:

1. Family Enterprise Institute™ (FEI) membership

2. FEI Business seminars, round tables and opportunities to network with other family owned businesses

3. FEI newsletter, **The Family Enterprise Institute™ Journal**

4. Business planning: Defining your real goals

5. Building investment value in your family-owned business

6. Using outside advisors to reach your goals

7. Marketing your business effectively

8. Navigating family relationships within the family business

9. Non-owner management techniques and how to use them

10. Passing your legacy on: Owner transition and retirement planning

11. Other:_____